A New Desire

Also by Brenda J. Robinson

Seized For His Glory

A New Desire Devotional

(A 365-Day Daily Devotional)

It Is Finished

A Victorious Christian Life

Made Over

Restructuring Your World (Adult Edition)

Restructuring Your World
      (Young Adult Edition)
      Co-written W/ Brooke Cason

Time in the Garden : Making His Heart Mine
      (A Family Devotional)
      Living and Leaving a Legacy
      Brenda and Dan Robinson
      Brooke and Labron Cason

A New Desire

Sailing Six Ships into Deep Channels of God's Sufficiency

Brenda J. Robinson

CROSSBOOKS
PUBLISHING

CrossBooks™
A Division of LifeWay
1663 Liberty Drive
Bloomington, IN 47403
www.crossbooks.com
Phone: 1-866-879-0502

First published by CrossBooks 3/27/2012

ISBN: 978-1-4627-1420-9 (hc)
ISBN: 978-1-4627-1419-3 (sc)
ISBN: 978-1-4627-1464-3 (e)

Library of Congress Control Number: 2012904392

Printed in the United States of America

This book is printed on acid-free paper.

Hope deferred maketh the heart sick: but when the desire cometh, it is a tree of life.

—Proverbs 13:12

Contents

Foreword

As a husband, father, and pastor, I am so thankful for the writing ministry of Dr. Brenda Robinson. Her study, *A New Desire*, has definitely left a mark on my household and on my congregation. It is easy for me to highly recommend to you something that has been tried and proven in my personal life. I have witnessed my wife, my two teenage daughters, and countless other ladies and girls be impacted by this work. Dr. Robinson has a God-given gift to write in a way that connects to the heart of the reader. In this study, she writes very passionately, practically, and powerfully. And men, this book is not just for the ladies; it will take a real man to work through this study and allow God to work in his life and make him a better man. However you choose to use this book, whether it is in a discipleship class, a couples' study, a family devotion, or just your own personal study, it's my prayer that God works in you as He has Dr. Robinson.

—*Bro. Chris Guinn, Pastor Crossville First Baptist Church; Crossville, AL*

Preface

Hope deferred maketh the heart sick: but when the desire cometh, it is a tree of life.

—Proverbs 13:12

This work is the result of a ten-year endeavor. It began with individual speeches and articles I wrote and submitted to newsletters and magazines. Then, after witnessing the life-changing results for those who attended the conferences and retreats or read the articles, God revealed to me that which was to be one of my greatest works yet.

This 6 week study contains a summary of all the lessons I have learned, the studies I have done, and the victory I have won. It is evidence of God's wonder-working power and His transforming grace—not only in my life but also in the lives of those who may now partake of this work.

After many years of wandering in the world, I came to realize that there had to be more to life than I was experiencing. My experiences brought me to a destitute place—a place where I found myself broken and hopeless. Questions plagued my mind, doubts filled my heart, and the enemy had stolen the motivation and desire to live that I had once possessed, thus, the reason for the title of this book, A New Desire. I would find myself sitting by a body of water, watching ships drift into uncharted territory, where doubt, fear, and the need for guidance was apparent.

In a desperate fight to survive, I came to realize that I ran my ship aground. I had allowed issues of doubt, disobedience to God's will, and lack of worship to toss my ship into the barnacles of life. Like these ships, I was unstable, drifting with the wind, longing for deeper channels of God's sufficiency. I did not have the power to win my battle. I was too weak in my flesh and too dry in my spirit. After years of struggling in the flesh, I awoke one day totally defeated, lacking even the desire to go on living. What would I do? How could I survive this dilemma? Was there any way out of the raging current? Through these questions and in the Word of God, I found *a new desire*, the motivation to escape my old way of life, and hope of a better way. In Proverbs 13:12, the Bible says, "Hope deferred maketh the heart sick: but when the desire cometh, it is a tree of life." This Scripture became my oasis, my motivation, and my hope.

My desire now is to teach others how to embrace *a new desire*—far above anything this life has to offer—in their own hearts. I'm speaking of a desire that will transform your heart and mind from a life of worldliness to one of righteousness and peace.

As Christians, we often base the depth of our spirituality on how often we feel God's presence or how much He blesses our lives. If we go two or three months without some great spiritual experience or blessing, we start questioning our closeness with God. We find ourselves drifting outside of God's will as we look for a quick fix for our discontentment. As Christians, we must move beyond these temporary experiences and develop a permanent relationship with God. This creates in us *a new desire* to serve God daily and to experience His grace and blessings.

A permanent relationship with God is based on how well you know Him. Therefore, it is our responsibility to develop an intimacy with Him by spending time in His Word, communicating with Him through prayer, and dissecting our own lives to remove the things in us that hinder an intimacy with Christ Jesus. Won't you join me in developing a new desire in your own life today?

Leader Guide

You as a leader are gifted with many spiritual gifts. You have developed some gifts more than others, and continue in obedience to study the living Word that shapes your life for His purpose.

Our ministry team is devoted to lift you to our Father, as you prepare these lessons, and I want you to know that my heart longs to co-labor alongside you as you teach this material.

I pray that you will teach this material with passion, not because I am the Author, but because it directs each person to God's "Deep Channel of Sufficiency," through the truth of the knowledge and wisdom of His Word. Always know that His Word is absolute, it never changes, and you can always trust it and stand firm on its foundation.

Guard this gift of teaching that is entrusted to you, and never take it for granted, but deliver it through much prayer and reverence for the One who extends His grace and mercy. Know that you as a leader have been chosen to be an instrument of change for eternity, and for the sake of the Kingdom of God.

This study is rich in symbolism. As you prepare each week, keep in mind that a small symbolic token or even a word picture can add value to the student's memory retention. For example, our doubt can be symbolized by water that has no boundary. It has no usefulness. James 1:6 "But let him ask in faith, nothing wavering. For he that wavereth is like a wave of the sea driven with the wind and tossed." We are controlled by our surroundings. Water on the other hand can have great power if it is managed properly, it can turn the turbines in a great ship.

Make a biblical application. Our weak faith avails nothing when we doubt because of our circumstances, but when we allow ourselves to be directed by the truth of God's word, we are not concerned with self and the drama of our life. Our doubt can be channeled into depth and stability through our faith, being turned into blessings, with the power of the all-sufficient God flowing through us.

Leader, provide an inexpensive memento that will serve as a reminder to the students of the theme of the study. In this case, use a ship silhouette in your power point, or a ship clip art for a bookmark as a reminder of the Courtship that is developing in our relationship with Jesus the lover of our souls.

Developing the Courtship

Dealing with Doubt

Weekly Thought

*C*ourtship is "the act, process, or period of wooing". [1] Jesus longs to court those who seek a courtship with Him. His wooing began before the foundations of the world and was proven at Calvary. Jesus offers a love everlasting, a life more abundant, and a courtship that provides all that is His to "whosoever will."

"Come unto me, all ye that labour and are heavy laden, and I will give you rest. Take my yoke upon you, and learn of me; for I am meek and lowly in heart: and ye shall find rest unto your souls. For my yoke is easy, and my burden is light" (Matthew 11:28–30 KJV).

I f we have received Jesus Christ as Lord of our life, we automatically have a courtship with Him. A courtship is made up of three elements:[1]

---

1   Barnhart, Clarence L., Barnhart, Robert, eds. The World Book Dictionary. (Chicago, London, Sydney, Toronto: World Book, Inc., 1988), p. 478

⚓ the wooing
⚓ the attraction
⚓ the meeting

The Holy Spirit began wooing us long before we ever met Jesus. His wooing began before the foundation of the world, and it was demonstrated at Calvary. The moment we realized we were sinners, God was attracted to us. That's right; our sin got God's attention. No, God doesn't love sin, but He loves the sinner. Adam and Eve are a great example of sin, activating God's grace and mercy into their lives. (See Genesis 3:6-21.) It wasn't our beauty, our wealth, our social standing, or our worldly possessions. The day we cried, "Lord, save me," we were acknowledging the convicting power of the Holy Spirit's wooing. The meeting took place at the moment of salvation. We entered into a courtship when we called out to God, and God is always touched when we depend upon Him.

Jesus desires for us to partake in a courtship with Him to the point that we recognize His wooing in every aspect of our lives. He is ever faithful to be there for us when we slip and fall. He is gracious and compassionate toward our every need and pain. This is His love toward us. His wooing began while we were still sinners. Romans 5:6–8 says, "For when we were yet without strength, in due time Christ died for the ungodly. For scarcely for a righteous man will one die: yet peradventure for a good man some would even dare to die. But God commendeth his love toward us, in that, while we were yet sinners, Christ died for us." Jesus gave His life to draw us to Himself. This is the most precious type of courtship.

We also have a responsibility in this courtship. We are to love Christ as He loves us. We are to woo Him by living for Him in righteousness and sincerity. We are to magnify Him in all that we do. Romans 5:9–11 says, "Much more then, being now justified by his blood, we shall be saved from wrath through him. For if, when we were enemies, we were reconciled to God by the death of his Son, much more, being reconciled, we shall be saved by his life. And not only so, but we also joy in God through our Lord Jesus Christ, by whom we have now received the atonement." Justification through the Blood of Christ reconciles us to God; therefore, magnifying Christ should be our first priority. Magnifying Christ not only develops the courtship that will make us pleasing to God but also pours out upon us blessings far above our expectations.

Living for God is the attraction that develops the courtship. The wooing is the foundation for developing the courtship. If we seek God, He is pleased. If we love God, He is overjoyed. If we desire to serve Him, He is faithful to guide us into His service.

The most effective element of an intimate courtship with God (or anyone else) is the amount of time we spend with that person one on one. Conversely, doubt is the most devastating element in a relationship. Doubt produces fear, insecurities, and feelings of unworthiness. These issues, in turn, threaten and weaken the courtship. A small amount of doubt can destroy what great volumes of time have painstakingly built. For this reason, when doubt comes to plague us, we must deal with it swiftly and scripturally.

Day 1: The Issues of Doubt

Why do we struggle with serving God and depending upon Him for our every need? Why can't we accept God's unconditional love for us? What is the key problem that prevents us from developing a "courtship" with our loving Savior?

Jesus provided the answer in Matthew 14:31. He bade Peter to walk on the water. As Peter's faith grew weak, Jesus stretched forth His hand and defined the problem with these words: "O thou of little faith, wherefore didst thou doubt?" We must realize that our greatest problem in developing a "courtship" with God derives from the same doubt that Peter experienced. We must deal with three areas of doubt: (1) the doubt of our *position*, (2) the doubt of our *condition*, and, finally, (3) the doubt of our *abilities*.

The Doubt of Our Position

This doubt produces questions like these: Where do I really stand with God? Does He really love me? Does He care about my problems? Why would God want a personal relationship with me?

Can you relate to any of these questions at this point in your life? If yes, write your questions on the lines below.

_____

_____

_____

_____

_____

The Doubt of Our Condition

This doubt produces insecurities exemplified in thoughts and questions like these: I'm too unworthy to serve God. I'm not good enough to be loved by God. Why would God use me when I've never done anything for Him? Why would God want a relationship with me after all I have done?

Which of these insecurities have surfaced in you lately? Write them below.

_____

_____

_____

_____

The Doubt of Our Abilities

Doubting our abilities produces fear of failure and provokes fearful thoughts like "I can't serve God—*not me!*" "I'm not qualified to serve," "What if I mess up?" "How can I be effective for God?" and "What if God *isn't* calling me to do this?"

These fears will steal our blessings. Do any of these thoughts sound like yours? If yes, write them below. If no, maybe you have one of your own fearful thoughts you need to record.

_____

_____

_____

_____

A New Desire

If you want to have a new desire for Jesus, study Luke 7:17–23 and record what you learn below.

_____

_____
_____
_____
_____
_____
_____
_____
_____

Daily Journal

Record what you have learned about yourself from today's lesson.

_____
_____
_____
_____
_____
_____
_____
_____

Day 2: Doubt, the Ultimate Weapon

Doubt is Satan's ultimate weapon for preventing us from having an intimate relationship with the Lord. If the Devil can make us doubt our secure position in Christ, we will become unstable in our relationship with Him. We will doubt our salvation, doubt God's love for us, and doubt our ability to serve Him.

In the Garden of Eden, Satan used the weapon of doubt against Eve. The fall of man began in Genesis 3:1—with a simple seed of doubt—as Satan said to Eve, "Yeah, hath God said, ye shall not eat of every tree of the garden?" At that very moment, Satan adulterated the "courtship" between God and Eve. He planted the seed of doubt, and Eve's desires were shifted from God's truths to Satan's lies. Satan approached Eve in a very subtle, tempting manner—and Eve fell prey to his tactics.

What does the word *subtle* mean to you?

Look up the definition of *subtle* in a dictionary and record below any differences between your definition and its true meaning.

What did you just learn about the subtlety of Satan? What seed of doubt has he planted within you in the past? Refuse to let Satan shift your desires from godliness. Deal with your doubts by taking them to God. When you give it to God, Satan has to flee. James 4:7 says, "Submit yourselves therefore to God. Resist the devil, and he will flee from you."

A New Desire

If you want to have a new desire for Jesus, study Luke 12:22–34. Record what you learn below.

_____

_____

_____

_____

_____

_____

Daily Journal

Record what you have learned about God and
about yourself from today's lesson.

_____

_____

_____

_____

_____

_____

_____

_____

_____

_____

Day 3: Dealing with Doubt

"And straightway Jesus constrained his disciples to get into a ship, and to go before him unto the other side, while he sent the multitudes away. And when he had sent the multitudes away, he went up into a mountain apart to pray: and when the evening was come, he was there alone. But the ship was now in the midst of the sea, tossed with waves: for the wind was contrary. And in the fourth watch of the night Jesus went unto them, walking on the sea. And when the disciples saw him walking on the sea, they were troubled, saying, It is a spirit; and they cried out for fear. But straightway Jesus spake unto them, saying, Be of good cheer; it is I; be not afraid. And Peter answered him and said, Lord, if it be thou, bid me come unto thee on the water. And he said, Come. And when Peter was come down out of the ship, he walked on the water, to go to Jesus. But when he saw the wind boisterous, he was afraid; and beginning to sink, he cried, saying, Lord, save me. And immediately Jesus stretched forth his hand, and caught him, and said unto him, O thou of little faith, wherefore didst thou doubt?"

— Matthew 14:22–31

The passage above finds the disciples in the middle of a storm. It says, "But straightway Jesus spake unto them, saying, 'Be of good cheer; it is I; be not afraid.'" The disciples were scared, both by the storm and by this man walking on the water. Jesus spoke to them, saying, "Be not afraid." Peter asked Jesus to bid him to come to Him on the water if He truly was the Lord. When Jesus bid him to come, Peter started out on the water in faith, strong and ready to follow the Lord's command.

As he walked a little farther, Peter became afraid of the circumstances around him and began to sink. Peter started out in the will of God, but he ended up in fear and doubt. God had given him the power to walk on water, but Peter allowed his insecurities to overcome God's will.

Many times we respond to God's will for our own lives in the same way Peter did. We are eager to know God's will for our lives, but we are afraid to act on it. Even if we do find the faith to begin the journey, we often let voices of doubt discourage us. They ask us questions like: "Are we sure this is really the right thing to do?" "Are we ready for all of this?" "Are we sure it was God telling us to go in this direction?" Doubt begins to set in, and we lose all hope that we will ever really know the will of God for our lives.

> *God can restore our hope if we will learn*
> *to seek Him in our state of doubt.*

James 1:5 says, "If any of you lack wisdom, let him ask of God, that giveth to all men liberally, and upbraideth not; and it shall be given him." Don't give up on God's will; instead, follow in faith!

We can learn great lessons on how to deal with our doubt through today's passages of Scripture. Why do you think Peter began to sink? it was because he failed to deal with his fear.

Can you relate to Peter? Are you failing to deal with your fears? List your fears below.

Study Second Timothy 1:7. What does this verse say about fear?

Fear always causes doubt. Peter saw the waves and felt the winds, and they caused him to become intimidated by their force. Instead of trusting Jesus when He told Peter to "be not afraid," Peter gave in to his own fears. Peter failed to deal with his fears, and the doubts in his mind began to control him. Peter began to sink. How could Peter have dealt with this fear? All he had to do was say, "Jesus, I'm afraid. The winds are boisterous, and the waves are high, but I'm going to just keep my eyes on You. I have faith in You that I can walk on this water."

Are your fears causing you to doubt?

_____

_____

List one way you know you could deal with your fear and doubt.

_____

_____

_____

Peter's circumstances intimidated him as much as his fears did. In Peter's mind, he could not see that God was greater than the wind and waves. For one brief moment, he forgot that Jesus had bid him to come. Therefore, he allowed his circumstances to control him instead of depending on Jesus to see him through the storm.

What circumstances are intimidating or controlling you?

_____

_____

Do you doubt that God is greater than your circumstances? God cares about your doubts, fears, and circumstances. He promises to be with you always, and He wants to comfort you with the words "Be not afraid." He is the same God to you that He was to Peter. He understands that doubt weakens your faith and confidence in Him.

*Don't be afraid to go to God
with your doubts.*

He knows our doubts already. We must never forget that God is all-knowing. God wants us to confess our doubts to Him. That's what Peter did when he cried, "Lord save me" (Matt. 14:30).

Did Peter's lack of faith disappoint Jesus?

_____

_____

Did Jesus know beforehand that Peter's faith would waver? (See Matt. 14:26.)

_____

_____

How did Jesus deal with Peter's doubt? (See Matt. 14:31.)

_____

_____

Just as Jesus stretched forth His hand in the midst of Peter's doubt, He also stretches it forth to us in the midst of our doubts. This experience of doubt taught Peter more about Jesus than he ever knew before. Peter stayed with Jesus instead of beating himself down with a sense of failure, and the Lord used Peter in a mighty way. If we want *a new desire*, we *must deal with* our doubt, and move forward in our courtship with Christ Jesus—just like Peter did.

We are the ones who control the level of courtship we have with Jesus. If we constantly battle doubt, then our courtship with Him is not very stable. Jesus knows our heart. Jesus already knows about all the doubt, fear, and confusion going on inside of us. Do not become a victim of doubt; do not let it hinder our courtship with Christ. The Holy Spirit is wooing us to God's truths and love for us through this study. I remind you again of the three elements that make up the courtship:

- ⚓ *The meeting.* Go to Christ just as you are.
- ⚓ *The attraction.* Give to Him your whole heart.
- ⚓ *The wooing.* Persuade Him with a life of righteousness.

A New Desire

If you want to have *a new desire* for Jesus, study Mark 11:20–26 for yourself. Record what you learn below.

Daily Journal

Record what you have learned about God and
about yourself from today's lesson.

Day 4: The Principles of Doubting

"If any of you lacks wisdom, let him ask of God, who gives to all liberally and without reproach, and it will be given to him. But let him ask in faith, with no doubting, for he who doubts is like a wave of the sea driven and tossed by the wind."

—James 1:5–6, NKJV

Two biblical examples of doubt stand out above all others. One is Zacharias; the other is Thomas. Their stories reveal to us the principles of doubting that can make a great difference in our walk with God.

Zacharias doubted the message the angel brought to him from God. God promised to give Zacharias and Elizabeth a child, but Zacharias failed to believe God's promise. Immediately, Zacharias was made unable to speak because of his doubt. Thomas, on the other hand, received no punishment for his failure to believe the other disciples when they told him their Savior lived. What made Thomas's doubt different from Zacharias's?

First, Thomas's doubt was a learning experience for him; it was part of his growth. Zacharias's doubt was simply a lack of faith in God's power to do what seemed impossible. Second, Thomas's doubt was a temporary doubt based on what he had heard from man. Zacharias had been praying for a child for many years and had allowed himself to become so rooted in doubt about God's ability or desire to answer his prayer that he didn't believe, even though God sent an angel to give him the good news. Thomas, on the other hand, had learned not to put his trust in man alone. Thomas's doubt was more of a need for divine reassurance than a lack of belief.

A New Desire

Doubting is safe as long as we allow
it to be a learning process.

When we are in doubt, we should go to God for assurance, just like Thomas did. Don't let yourself dwell in doubt like Zacharias did. Today's Scripture text says, "If any of you lack wisdom, let him ask of God, that giveth to all men liberally, and upbraideth not; and it shall be given him. But let him ask in faith, nothing wavering." Seek God's will and rest in it!

Satan's tactic is for us to feel a sense of failure because of our doubts. If he can get our attention directed toward our failure rather than the lesson God wants to teach us, then he has accomplished his task. You see, Satan wants us to become more like Zacharias in our doubts. He wants us to direct our desires toward other things besides God's will and plan for our life. Therefore, he will tell us lies and make us believe them. He will make us doubt God's voice, just like Zacharias did, and then God will be forced to chasten (correct or discipline) us because of our unbelief. Hebrews 12:6 says, "For whom the Lord loveth he chasteneth, and scourgeth every son whom he receiveth."

What are you in unbelief about at this point in our life?

_____

_____

_____

_____

_____

_____

_____

Do you feel that God has already started the chastening process because of our unbelief?

_____

_____

_____

_____

What are some of the lies Satan has led you to believe in your time of doubt?

_____

_____

_____

How is our doubt affecting our witness for Christ?

_____

_____

_____

God chose Zacharias to be the father of John the Baptist. Zacharias's doubt and unbelief could have hindered God's plan of salvation, but God knew how to protect Zacharias from being defeated in his doubt. God had power over Zacharias. In spite of Zacharias's unbelief, God knew that Zacharias was the man who needed to father John the Baptist, who prepared the way for Jesus. The principle of doubt we must learn from Zacharias is that doubt should never be a root of defeat; rather, it should be the seed of growth.

List something that you have doubts about.

_____

_____

_____

Has your doubt become a root of defeat or a seed of growth?

_____

....

....

....

Zacharias's doubt could have cost him his blessing, but God, in His infinite plan, took Zacharias's doubt and taught him the principle of victory over doubt. So many times we are like Zacharias. The Lord speaks to us and shows us His will for our lives, but because of our circumstances, we just can't see how God could do something through us. Like Zacharias, we give God a list of "buts" and "what ifs."

What was the first "but" that Zacharias used? (See Luke 1:18.)

....

....

What are the "buts" or "what ifs" you are giving the Lord to compensate for the doubts you are dwelling in?

....

....

....

List one thing you *know* God has called you to do but that you have allowed doubt to detain you from doing.

....

....

The principle of doubt we learn from Zacharias is that doubting what we know God has called us to do and then dwelling in the doubt brings upon us correction and discipline. God was faithful to reassure Zacharias by sending the angel Gabriel to speak to him personally, yet Zacharias still chose to doubt the voice of God. God allowed Zacharias to doubt, but then, to protect Zacharias from defeat, God made His presence and His will known by making him unable to speak.

God always makes Himself known in such
a way that all doubts are resolved.

As we studied earlier, Zacharias doubted God's angel, and Thomas doubted man. The Bible states in Luke 1:6 that Zacharias and his wife Elisabeth "were both righteous before God, walking in all the commandments and ordinances of the Lord blameless." Zacharias was strong in faith. However, his longstanding desire for a child and the issue of his advanced age had fostered unbelief in him that only God could remove. Zacharias's weakness of faith hindered his courtship with God. God knew Zacharias's heart. Therefore, God could not allow Zacharias's doubt to go on any longer. Zacharias had always been rooted in God, but this one desire had controlled him to the point that it was difficult for him to even believe an angel of the Lord. Thomas, on the other hand, had a tendency to always doubt everything. He was known as a man who had to see it before he believed it. He had a hard time believing *anything* man had to say. However, Thomas did not dwell in his doubt. He always sought to find the truth by asking questions and seeking proof (John 20:25).

Jesus was always quick to respond to Thomas's doubt. He is faithful to respond to our doubts too. We must pursue Him for the truth. When we seek Him, as Thomas did, we will learn from our doubts. We will experience God, and our desires to serve Him will subdue any doubts we may face.

Thomas was a "show me" kind of disciple. Once Jesus reassured his doubts, I don't believe Thomas ever doubted that particular issue again. You see, Thomas was faithless where Zacharias was weak in faith. There is a big difference between *weakness* of faith and being totally *faithless.* Someone who is weak in faith has experienced the power of God and knows deep in his heart that God can do the impossible. However, he allows his circumstances to overpower his faith. Someone who is faithless has to live by sight; he is very often the unbeliever or the believer who has a problem trusting God or His Word.

Jesus revealed His mind on this matter to Thomas in John 20:27: "Then saith he to Thomas, Reach hither thy finger, and behold my hands; and reach hither thy hand, and thrust it into my side: and be not faithless, but believing." Where does your doubt have you? Are you faithless or just weak in faith?

_____

_____

_____

_____

Are you a Zacharias or a Thomas in your state of doubt? Have you learned from these examples the *principles of doubting*? List what you have learned.

_____

_____

We can learn a lot about doubt from Thomas and Zacharias. There are several positives to be seen about their times of doubt that you can apply to your own situation:

1. They never gave up on God.
2. They learned new things about God.
3. In their doubting, they learned more about themselves.
4. As they worked through their doubt, they developed a greater trust in God.

Challenge yourself to study the Bible to see how many different Scriptures you can find in which people experienced doubt. List those people and their responses to doubt below.

_____

_____

_____

Below, list the most recent examples of doubt in your own life.

Beside each one, record Zacharias's or Thomas's name according to the way in which you responded.

_____

_____

_____

_____

_____

Note what *you* have learned while working through (with God) the seasons of doubt you have experienced.

_____

_____

_____

_____

_____

_____

_____

_____

A New Desire

If you want to have a new desire for Jesus, study James 1:1–12 for yourself. Record what you learn below.

_____

_____

_____

_____

Daily Journal

Record what you have learned about God and
about yourself from today's lesson.

_____

_____

_____

_____

_____

_____

_____

Day 5: Defying Doubt

"Being confident of this very thing, that he which hath begun a good work in you will perform it until the day of Jesus Christ."

—Philippians 1:6

Defying doubt means to resist it or openly and boldly oppose it. If we are going to have an intimate courtship with Jesus Christ, we must boldly oppose the voice of doubt. We cannot build a relationship with God or anyone else if there is no trust. Doubt automatically makes us untrusting.

Don't let doubt dwell in your life. We've already learned that God will give us the wisdom to deal with our doubts. Secure yourself in His will, and then do God's will without looking back at the doubts.

Choosing to live for God always brings doubt. Doubt is one of Satan's finest weapons. Satan knows that if he can place doubt in our mind, then we are a target for deception. However, we can overcome if we know God's will for our life.

Our doubts about God's will can be resolved by reading God's Word. God's Word is His voice to us, and we can depend on it to verify God's will.

God will give us the wisdom to
deal with our doubts.

Thomas doubted God's plan when he heard it from man, but when Thomas got the message from God, he never doubted again. We should handle our doubts just as Thomas did. Seek God's Word, listen for His voice, and trust Him.

We should confidently serve God and praise Him for using us. Our Scripture text for today says, "Being confident of this very thing, that

He which hath begun a good work in you will perform it until the day of Jesus Christ." If God began a work in you, He will be faithful to finish it. If you are a born-again child of God, you have a power inside of you that will not let you quit on God. That power is the Holy Spirit within you. He will never leave you nor forsake you; He will guide you in your work for the Lord.

When Peter walked on the water, he began to doubt, "And immediately Jesus stretched forth his hand, and caught him, and said unto him, O thou of little faith, wherefore didst thou doubt?" (Matt. 14:31). Jesus' hand is stretched out to you now. Defy the doubt, and take His hand!

What have you learned about doubt and its effects in this week's lessons?

_____

_____

_____

_____

_____

_____

_____

_____

Consult a dictionary. What is the definition of *defy*?

_____

_____

_____

A New Desire

If you want to have a new desire for Jesus, study Judges 6:11–40 for yourself. Record what you learn below.

_____

_____

_____

_____

_____

_____

_____

Daily Journal

Record what you have learned about God and
about yourself from today's lesson.

_____

_____

_____

_____

_____

_____

_____

_____

Establishing the Relationship
A Disciplined Prayer Life

Weekly Thought

*H*aving a relationship means, "having a connection; it is the condition of belonging to the same family as someone else." [1] Galatians 4:4–7 says, "But when the fullness of time was come, God sent forth his Son, made of a woman, made under the law, to redeem them that were under the law, that we might receive the adoption of sons. And because ye are sons, God hath sent forth the Spirit of his Son into our hearts, crying, Abba, Father. Wherefore thou art no more a servant, but a son; and if a son, then an heir of God through Christ."

The Word of God explicitly defines the relationship right here in these Scriptures. Jesus gave His life and became the sacrifice. We receive the adoption through salvation, thus forming a relationship that can never be severed.

The key to developing a right relationship with God is in the five little words of Galatians 4:6. It says, *"And because ye are sons."* The

---

1   Barnhart, Clarence L., Barnhart, Robert, eds. The World Book Dictionary. (Chicago, London, Sydney, Toronto: World Book, Inc., 1988), p. 1764

only means of a relationship with God is through His Son Jesus Christ. Accepting Christ into our hearts makes us sons, and because we are sons, we can have the deepest, most intimate relationship with Jesus Christ. The quality and value of any relationship comes through choice. We choose the depth of our relationship by what we are willing to put into it. God chose to love us before the foundations of the world. Therefore, He chose to begin a relationship with us. Because of Christ's example, we find that an intimate relationship is based on three essentials:

⚓ the choice
⚓ the commitment
⚓ the communication

Just as Christ chose to love us and die for our sins, we too must choose a life of righteousness over a life of worldliness and rebellion. We choose whether or not we want to walk with the Lord. Oftentimes we choose a shallow, surface relationship rather than intimacy with God by refusing to turn from the worldliness that distracts us from the righteousness of God.

The choices we make in life determine just how committed we will be in our walk with God. It is natural for us to be dedicated to our jobs, yet it's so hard for us to commit ourselves to God's work. Too often we base our dedication to God's service on what we can get out of it. If it comes with little recognition or money, then God's work and our relationship with Him are not our top priority. If our commitment to God is not up to par, then our communication will be lacking too.

With choice comes commitment and communication. Choice, commitment, and communication work together to make an intimate relationship. Communication is the key ingredient for strength and stability in any relationship. Lack of communication means lack of intimacy. To enjoy the full rewards of intimacy with God, we must devote ourselves to a life of communication with our Lord and Savior, Jesus Christ.

Still, we often harbor inner thoughts, feelings, and questions about God, thinking God doesn't know about them. Confession is communication. It does not matter if we are harboring anger, rebellion, confusion, etc. The key to a relationship with Christ is telling Him from our hearts how we feel and what we are thinking and then seeking Him for the answers to our questions. This, my friend, is how we develop a disciplined prayer life.

Prayer is simply communicating with God. If we make the choice to pray and then commit ourselves to that choice, communication automatically develops a personal relationship with Jesus that will cause us to be found faithful in His sight.

Second Chronicles 7:14–15 verifies this truth for us. It says, "If my people, which are called by my name, shall humble themselves, and pray, and seek my face, and turn from their wicked ways; then will I hear from heaven, and will forgive their sin, and will heal their land. Now mine eyes shall be open, and mine ears attentive unto the prayer that is made in this place."

Day 1: Effective Prayer

(Nehemiah's Example)

A disciplined prayer life begins with the realization that prayer does not require proper words or ceremonial acts. Prayer is simply a confidential courtship between you and God, and it establishes an intimate relationship that makes God very real in your life.

Prayer proves that we have a
desire to know God's will.

As we communicate with God, He is faithful to hear our supplications. We can talk to God just as we talk to our best friends. We can have that kind of relationship with Him. God does not require long, graceful speeches when we make our petitions known to Him. Nehemiah's prayer in Nehemiah 1:6–11 is a great example of a God-honored prayer. It says:

> "Let thine ear now be attentive, and thine eyes open, that thou mayest hear the prayer of thy servant, which I pray before thee now, day and night, for the children of Israel thy servants, and confess the sins of the children of Israel, which we have sinned against thee: both I and my father's house have sinned. We have dealt very corruptly against thee, and have not kept the commandments, nor the statutes, nor the judgments, which thou commandedst thy servant Moses. Remember, I beseech thee, the word that thou commandedst thy servant Moses, saying, If ye transgress, I will scatter you abroad among the nations: But if ye turn unto me, and keep my commandments, and do them; though there were of you cast out unto the uttermost part of the heaven, yet will I gather them

from thence, and will bring them unto the place that I have chosen to set my name there. Now these are thy servants and thy people, whom thou hast redeemed by thy great power, and by thy strong hand. O Lord, I beseech thee, let now thine ear be attentive to the prayer of thy servant, and to the prayer of thy servants who desire to fear thy name: and prosper, I pray thee, thy servant this day, and grant him mercy in the sight of this man. For I was the king's cupbearer."

Wow, what a prayer! Let's study Nehemiah's example and learn the keys to effective prayer from it.

Nehemiah pretty much covered everything on his heart in these few verses. He not only confessed his sin to God, but in verses eight and nine, he even reminded God of His promise to His people way back in the day of Moses. From this prayer, we can see that Nehemiah had certainly established a right relationship with God. This man was in dire need. He needed to get in touch with God, and he knew exactly how to do it. He had overcome any doubts he might have had about the proper way to pray. He lived with the blessed assurance and confidence that God hears all of our prayers, whether they are systematic or spontaneous. Nehemiah had an inner security that his prayer life was both disciplined and powerful.

Do you have an inner security that God hears your prayers? If not, list below the causes of your insecurity.

When you pray, do you have doubts that God is listening? If yes, list the issues that cause your doubt on the lines below.

When you pray, do you hear voices of negativity or experience feelings of unworthiness? Check the box that best relates to you.

- ❑ Yes, I hear voices of negativity.
- ❑ Yes, I experience unworthiness.
- ❑ I experience both.
- ❑ I experience neither.

When you have a desire to pray, do you experience any of the *inner voices* below? Check the box or boxes that best relate to you.

- ❑ Why pray now? You don't pray when times are good.
- ❑ Prayer is silly.
- ❑ You don't need to pray about that.
- ❑ God doesn't care about you.
- ❑ God has much bigger and more important issues to deal with.
- ❑ Someone might see you praying and think something's wrong.
- ❑ God is not going to hear your prayer because of that sin you committed.
- ❑ You don't have time to pray; you need to get this done first.
- ❑ If you pray now, someone might come in or the phone may ring. You need to wait until later.
- ❑ This is not the time or the place for you to be praying.

Do you give in to the voices above and carry on without praying?

- ❑ Sometimes
- ❑ Most of the time
- ❑ Every time
- ❑ Never

Do you think Nehemiah allowed negative voices to hinder his communication with God?

According to Nehemiah's approach to God, would you say Nehemiah thought God had a memory lapse of what He said He would do, or was he making a plea for God to activate what He promised?

Nehemiah 1:6a says, "Let thine ear now be attentive, and thine eyes open ..." What is the first thing Nehemiah had to do for his prayer to be effective?

In Nehemiah 1:6b, what words of Nehemiah attracted God to hear and set His eyes upon Nehemiah's prayer?

In verse 9a, what does it say that God requires of His people before He will honor His promise?

In the closing of Nehemiah's prayer, what three requirements must we fulfill to have the inner security that God is attentive to our prayers?

According to today's study, how effective is your prayer life?

_____

_____

_____

_____

A New Desire

If you want to have a new desire for Jesus, study James 5:13–18 for yourself. Record what you learn below.

_____

_____

_____

_____

Daily Journal

Record what you have learned about God and
about yourself from today's lesson.

_____

_____

_____

_____

_____

_____

Day 2: Three Steps to a Disciplined Prayer Life.

In today's study, we are going to discover just what it takes to be disciplined in our prayer lives and our relationships with God. According to Matthew 6:6, there are three things we can do to obtain a disciplined prayer relationship with our heavenly Father. Let's find out what these three steps are so that we can experience a new desire in our walk of righteousness.

Matthew 6:6 says, "But thou, when thou prayest, enter into thy closet, and when thou hast shut thy door, pray to thy Father which is in secret; and thy Father which seeth in secret shall reward thee openly." The three steps are found in this one small verse. They are the following:

1. Enter into your closet.
2. Shut the door.
3. Pray in secret.

In Matthew 6:6 and many other Scriptures throughout the Bible, God teaches us the important principles for our prayer life. Prayer is essential in the life of every believer. Prayer must become the very breath of our lives, and we must discipline ourselves to pray every day. A healthy prayer life always has great rewards; we are told this in the verse above.

When we pray with discipline, God is able to speak to us about matters we wouldn't normally think He cares about.

God is concerned about the most minute parts of our lives, even the material things. God always wants the best for His children, but He can't teach us this principle until we get personal with Him.

Prayer was given to us for many reasons, but the most important is to know God more intimately. God already knows all about us. Our prayer life teaches us about His will for our lives and draws us closer to Him.

A disciplined prayer life requires us to do several things. First, we must enter into our closet. Our closet is any place that is private, away from all distractions. Our closet is a place where we can be alone with God. We will form a very private prayer life with the Lord. It is time for us as Christians to develop this type of intimacy with Christ. Find a place to call your *closet,* and get personal with God today! The word closet in the original Greek means a place for storage and privacy or *a secret chamber.*

Where is your secret chamber, and what do you need to store there?

_____

_____

_____

Name the Old Testament prophet who prayed three times a day.

_____

_____

_____

In what position did this prophet pray?

_____

_____

Daniel's intimate relationship with God was developed through his prayer life. Daniel's discipline gave him power and confidence. He knew God was the only true God, and no man could shake his faith.

A disciplined prayer life requires oneness with God.

Giving God our *undivided* attention produces a very personal relationship. When we get personal with God, we get results from our prayers. Daniel had this personal, private place of prayer, and he got results from his prayers. The secret chamber works every time!

The second and third steps to a disciplined prayer life are to "shut thy door, [and] pray to thy Father which is in secret." You must "shut the door." The door here refers to closing our minds to all other thoughts while opening our hearts to the presence of God. When we shut the door of our minds, we allow God room to come in and saturate our hearts with His love and instructions.

Many times when we pray, we pray from our minds instead of our hearts. This is why people's prayers are seldom effective; they pray with minds full of vain and selfish requests. God will never honor selfish, gain-seeking prayers. We get results when we pray with an empty mind and an open heart because God is then able to transform our minds.

How long has it been since you examined your prayer life? Start praying with your door shut today. Close your mind to your circumstances. Pray to the Father with an open heart. You will surely be blessed by His presence and provision for you. When you pray with an open heart, you will find yourself laying your circumstances at the feet of Jesus.

What is the latest prayer God has answered for you?

How did you respond to the answered prayer?

Was it the answer you wanted? If not, write what you wanted God to do instead?

Where was one of Jesus' secret places to pray? (See Matt. 26.)

For what did Jesus make three requests to His Father in this passage of Scripture?

Was Jesus' prayer answered in the way He asked for it to be?

What was Jesus' response in Matthew 26:42?

Jesus is Himself the greatest example of a person with a disciplined prayer life. His relationship with His Father as He walked on this earth was established and maintained through a personal prayer life. Let's follow Christ's example—*and pray!*

A New Desire

If you want to have a new desire for Jesus, study Matthew 6:5–15 for yourself. Record what you learn below.

_____

_____

_____

_____

_____

Daily Journal

Record what you have learned about God and
about yourself from today's lesson.

_____

_____

_____

_____

_____

_____

_____

Day 3: Types of Prayer

Systematic and Spontaneous Prayer

For the next few days, I want to share with you the elements of four different types of prayers. Together we will learn how and when to apply each type of prayer to make our lives for Christ flourish. Regardless of the type of prayer, Mark 11:24 tells us what makes each effective. It says, "Therefore I say unto you, What things soever ye desire, when ye pray, believe that ye receive them, and ye shall have them."

So often we live defeated Christian lives because of our insecurities about doing things correctly in the eyes of God. Do we witness, study, and pray in the approved manner? We need to learn to be like Nehemiah. We need to overcome our doubts and insecurities about whether we're praying correctly. God hears and answers every prayer of faith. He may not answer in the way we want Him to, but He hears and answers nevertheless.

> *We see in our Scripture text for today that an effective prayer life is the key to overcoming and achieving all things in our Christian walk.*

There are four types of prayer. They are as follows:

1. systematic prayer
2. spontaneous prayer
3. specific prayer
4. serious prayer

None of these types of prayer is more effective than the others. They're all effective when they're prayed in faith. Let's learn about each type so we can have more confidence in our prayers.

Systematic Prayer

The first type of prayer is *Systematic*. What is systematic prayer, and is it good or bad? Systematic prayers are those prayers that we usually rush through just for the sake of saying them, like a blessing at each meal. We often say them just to be released from the guilt of forgetfulness and carelessness. Saying a systematic prayer also makes us feel good about ourselves because it can make us look "*holy.*"

Jesus said in Matthew 6:7, "But when ye pray, use not vain repetitions, as the heathen do: for they think that they shall be heard for their much speaking." God condemns shallow, traditional prayers that are not from the heart.

Does this mean that we would be better off to skip those meal blessings? *No,* it does not. We should simply be more aware of what we are doing.

> *Our prayers, for any reason,*
> *should be sincere before God.*

Prayer should come from a sincere heart. God commends persistent prayer. He doesn't tire of hearing us say a blessing at each meal; He tires of hearing us say the same prayer at each meal that we've said every day for every meal just because we're supposed to say it. God doesn't even mind hearing the same words over and over again as long as they're said with sincerity. Jesus made prayer a continuous habit. Luke 11:1 says, "And it came to pass, that, as he was praying in a certain place, when he ceased, one of his disciples said unto him, Lord, teach us to pray, as John also taught his disciples." It is very important that we discipline ourselves in the habit of prayer. If Jesus had need of a "certain place," don't you think we need that as well?

The disciples were prayer warriors, but we must understand their desire to take on prayer as a habit. They said, "Lord, teach us to pray." The disciples had been with Jesus for approximately three years, and they had observed everything about His prayer life. They not only observed His prayers, but they also observed the results of His prayers. Still, Jesus was faithful to teach His disciples how to pray. In Matthew

6:9–13, He gave the model and systematic prayer commonly referred to as the Lord's Prayer.

According to what you have just studied, are you *effective* or tra*ditional* in your systematic prayers?

_____

_____

_____

Are most of your systematic prayers recited from those you've heard over the years (e.g., your meal blessings, your bedtime prayers, etc.). If yes, please keep in mind that these types of prayers are not wrong. God honors each prayer we pray as long as we pray in sincerity. Keep praying them! God honors our communication with Him.

_____

_____

In Matthew 6:7, what do the words "vain repetition" mean?

_____

_____

_____

Systematic prayer is always heard by the Lord. However, it is important that we stay mindful of who we are approaching when we pray. God knows the sincerity of our prayers, and meaningless words said out of habit and tradition are not honored by an omniscient God. Systematic prayer often becomes simply a pretty prayer with no action. The same prayer said from the heart rather than from memory or tradition can touch heaven. Discipline your prayer life to one of sincerity, and you may see great results even from a systematic prayer!

Spontaneous Prayers

What is *spontaneous* prayer? It is an immediate, desperate, emergency call from a child of God who needs immediate care, provision, and attention from his Father. Nehemiah is our biblical example of spontaneous prayer. Nehemiah had approached King Artaxerxes for permission to return to Jerusalem and rebuild the city walls. Nehemiah was afraid to approach the king. However, when the king asked, "For what dost thou make request?" Nehemiah called out to God in a spontaneous prayer for guidance.

As we read in Nehemiah 2, the king granted Nehemiah permission to return to Jerusalem. Obviously, spontaneous prayer can be very productive, but what we ask for must still be in agreement with God's will. Whatever we ask for, and however we ask for it, must ultimately be intended to uplift Jesus Christ.

We should also be spiritually prepared to receive whatever we ask for spontaneously. We often exercise impulsive prayers to escape an uncomfortable situation we are not prepared to handle. In these situations, we should evaluate our purpose for prayer. Perhaps we should examine all of our spontaneous prayers to see the true intention of our hearts. If we pray on the spur of the moment, we often expect the answer on the spur of the moment. If we are not spiritually rooted in Christ Jesus, this could lead to problems. If the answer does not come immediately, we become weak in the faith and open to Satan's deceptions.

In order to practice effective spontaneous prayer, we must first learn to exercise spiritual maturity by applying faith even to our spontaneous prayers.

James 1:6 says, "But let him ask in faith, nothing wavering. For he that wavereth is like a wave of the sea driven with the wind and tossed."

Don't waver in faith just because your prayer is spontaneous. Believe that God hears your prayer just because it's a prayer of faith. Don't let the enemy prevent you from praying spontaneously by telling you that you're supposed to pray in a certain position and close your eyes. Nehemiah did not have time to shut his eyes, bow on his knees, or find a private place. He had to move quickly; that's why the Scripture says, "So I prayed to the God of heaven." We *must learn to activate spontaneous faith like Nehemiah did so that when we "pray to the God of heaven,"* we can believe He will come to our rescue.

The best way to deal with the fiery darts of the enemy is to abide by Ephesians 6:18, which says, "Praying always with all prayer and supplication in the Spirit, and watching thereunto with all perseverance and supplication for all saints." You see, the fervent shield of prayer can be used whenever and wherever. We have online access to heaven. We can pray over anything at any time—on our jobs, in our homes, over our families, and on the road. We can even pray when we have a hundred things going on at one time, spontaneously making our requests and expressing our desires a thousand times a day!

In Matthew 8:25, what was the disciples' emergency?

Did Jesus respond immediately?

In Matthew 14:30, what was Peter's emergency?

What words did Peter pray?

When and how did Jesus respond to Peter's prayer?

How many times have you prayed an immediate, "Lord, save me"?

Did He save you from the moment of desperation?

When you have needed God on the spur of a moment, how many times has the enemy told you God could not intervene that quickly?

Can you remember any specific time when you needed God spontaneously and He was there?

To receive the effects of spontaneous prayer, we must believe that the same God who works in our life yesterday, today, and tomorrow is working in the now of the situation we are currently facing.

I have learned in my personal experiences with God that I can spontaneously call upon Him for what *most* would consider minute issues. For example, I have learned to ask God to bestow immediate peace upon me when I am in turmoil or uncertainty. If I can feel His peace, then I am reassured of His presence in my situation.

Spontaneous prayer is not just effective—it is exciting! It should spark a new desire in us to know that God is honored to work in our immediate needs. If we have physical, mental, emotional, financial, family, marital, relational, social, or spiritual needs right now, at this very moment, we can pray a spontaneous prayer of help.

A New Desire

Find at least three examples in the Bible where the Lord was called on in an emergency, immediate situation. Record the three, and record the Lord's response to spontaneous prayer below.

_____

_____

_____

_____

_____

Daily Journal

Record what you have learned about God and prayer
from today's lesson. Did it stir a desire in you to learn
more or to study God's Word more often?

_____

_____

_____

_____

_____

_____

_____

_____

Day 4: Types of Prayer

Specific and Serious Prayers

Specific Prayer

Specific prayer is often the target of Satan's attacks because this type of prayer is the one we most often get confused about. Specific prayer can cause us to believe that we are praying selfishly. Matthew 21:22 is the key to defeating our foe on this. It says, "And all things, whatsoever ye shall ask in prayer, believing, ye shall receive." God wants us to pray. First Timothy 2:8 says, "I will therefore that men pray everywhere, lifting up holy hands, without wrath and doubting."

God is big and loving enough to give us whatever our hearts desire. However, God expects honesty and sincerity in specific prayer, just as He does with systematic and spontaneous prayer. Being able to ask God for specific things is a blessing and a benefit that comes with being a born-again child of God. God honors specific prayer that honors Him. God does not honor specific prayer to fulfill the lusts of our flesh. God will not answer prayer for things that will strain our relationships with Him or hinder our service for Him.

Nehemiah prayed for several specific things, and God heard and answered his prayers. Specific prayer is rewarding if we follow God's plan for prayer. Nothing pleases God more than to be able to reveal Himself to us by answering our prayers.

> *Specific prayer is the best way to see*
> *God in action.*

For the honor and glory of God, pray specifically, and watch God reveal Himself to you as the God who hears and answers prayer!

We can't go any further in our study of specific prayer without incorporating the final type of prayer: serious prayer. Specific prayer and serious prayer must be combined if we are to experience an effective line of communication with our heavenly Father.

As we stated above, Nehemiah's prayers were very specific, thus proving the seriousness of his request. Nehemiah's prayer was also serious prayer. All of our prayers, whether they be systematic, spontaneous, or specific, should be serious. If we would only pray seriously instead of worriedly, then we could have the same confidence in prayer that Nehemiah had.

We must put aside all of our doubts, fears, and confusions about how to pray properly and focus on the positive, serious side of prayer. If we pray at *all, we are praying correctly in God's eyes. It pleases God when we sacrifice* our time to talk with Him and trust Him in prayer.

To pray seriously simply means to recognize God as the Father, Jesus as the Son, and the Holy Spirit as the Comforter. Jesus gave His life for our sins so we could have access to the Father. His Holy Spirit guides us in prayer. Romans 8:26 says, "Likewise the Spirit also helpeth our infirmities: for we know not what we should pray for as we ought: but the Spirit itself maketh intercession for us with groanings which cannot be uttered."

Serious prayer requires us to set aside time each day to steal away somewhere to pray, meditate, and worship. Serious prayer consists of praying for the needs of others over our own needs and praying consistently until we've seen results.

> *Serious prayer is at its best when we can get*
> *on our knees before God just to praise Him*
> *and thank Him for all our blessings.*

Let's be like Nehemiah and get serious with God in prayer.

Can you recall a specific prayer you have prayed? If yes, what was God's response?

What does Matthew 21:22 tell us we must do to have our prayers answered?

_____

_____

_____

_____

According to our notes on serious prayer, what does praying seriously mean?

_____

_____

_____

_____

A New Desire

Find a specific circumstance in the Bible that is similar to what you are facing. Record that circumstance and the end results.

_____

_____

_____

_____

_____

Daily Journal

Start praying right now for your specific need.
Record that need below. Then record when the
prayer is answered and how God answered it.

Day 5: Renewing the Relationship

If we are ever going to understand and enjoy a relationship with Jesus Christ, we must see ourselves as He sees us. Jesus does not base His love on our abilities or accomplishments. He does not love us less because of our mistakes or failures. He loves us because that is His heart and His nature. First John 4:9–10 says, "In this was manifested the love of God toward us, because that God sent his only begotten Son into the world, that we might live through him. Herein is love, not that we loved God, but that he loved us, and sent his Son to be the propitiation for our sins."

Our relationship with Christ is built on the foundation of the love of God. If we love Christ as He loves us, then our relationship is pleasing and prosperous in the sight of God.

Love and prayer are the forces behind the level of communication we have with our Savior. Therefore, it is vitally important that we keep an open and sincere line of communication between God and ourselves.

Through this week's study, we have learned that we must have an unhindered, disciplined prayer life to have a right relationship with God. The more we communicate with God, the stronger we become. Prayer develops the relationship because when we pray, we are placing our faith and trust in Him. Prayer is the bond that seals and secures an intimacy with Jesus, our Lord.

When we lose our desire to serve the Lord and life appears hopeless, it is time to review our lives and examine our hearts. If we want to keep a close relationship with Christ, we must guard our hearts and minds against the world, Satan, and our own flesh. We have the Word of God to stand on in these times. However, it is important that we use the Word of God daily as our weapon of *offense* and *defense*.

God's Word is His form of communication with His children. He also communicates with us through His Holy Spirit and others. When we feel God is nowhere near us, it is time to renew our relationship with

Him. We can go to Him and tell Him everything we are experiencing because He knows it already. When we have burdens, we can take them to Him and lay them at His feet and know that He cares. God loves us that much!

Jesus revealed the heart relationship He had for His people in His prayer to His Father just before He went to the cross. In John 17, we not only see how deep His love for us is, but we also see an example of a disciplined, unhindered prayer life. Through Jesus' example of prayer, we can learn much about our own prayer lives and the depth of our relationship with Christ. Let's study Jesus' prayer and apply it to our own lives for a renewing of our relationship with Him. As we break this prayer down into sections, compare the way you pray to how Jesus prayed and learn from this example.

John 17:1–5 says:

> "These words spake Jesus, and lifted up his eyes to heaven, and said, Father, the hour is come; glorify thy Son, that thy Son also may glorify thee: As thou hast given him power over all flesh, that he should give eternal life to as many as thou hast given him. And this is life eternal, that they might know thee the only true God, and Jesus Christ, whom thou hast sent. I have glorified thee on the earth: I have finished the work which thou gavest me to do. And now, O Father, glorify thou me with thine own self with the glory which I had with thee before the world was."

There is a great deal to learn about the way Jesus prayed versus *our* mentality on praying. Notice in verse 1, Jesus lifted His eyes to heaven. We usually close our eyes to pray, and this is not wrong. However, it is plain to see through Jesus' example that we can pray with our eyes open and lifted to heaven. Closing our eyes represents humility and reverence to God almighty. Likewise, lifting our eyes to heaven represents confidence and boldness in approaching our heavenly Father.

The next thing that must be noted is that Jesus prayed for Himself. He said, "Glorify thy Son, that thy Son also may glorify thee." Jesus was not praying a boastful or prideful prayer. He was praying for Himself so His Father would be glorified through Him. We must be willing to glorify the Savior through our bodies. It is very important that we pray for ourselves so Jesus can be magnified. We are to confess our sins, ask for strength, and be willing to face things that are outside of our comfort zones.

Jesus also made another statement about Himself while He was praying. He said, "Glorify thou me with thine own self with the glory which I had with thee before the world was." Jesus was praying for His place with His Father around the throne where He was before the foundations of the world. Jesus was praying for His reward for finishing His work, and we can too.

The greatest prayer we can pray for ourselves is the prayer of dedication and commitment in the work that God has called us to do. Jesus grew tired of the battles and weary on His journey. He was rejected, abused, and abandoned, but He stayed faithful to the Father's call upon His life. From the first five verses of this prayer, we can see that it is God's will for us to pray for ourselves. If we fail to pray for ourselves first, then it is very possible that the rest of our prayer might be hindered!

The Bible teaches us to confess our sin, plead our cause, and admit to our mistakes, habits, hindrances, and weaknesses. We must get self out of the way and out in the open with God so we can have a renewed relationship with Him. Jesus always drew strength from His relationship with His Father.

Next Jesus prayed for His disciples. In verses 6–19 He said:

> "I have manifested thy name unto the men which thou gavest me out of the world: thine they were, and thou gavest them me; and they have kept thy word. Now they have known that all things whatsoever thou hast given me are of thee. For I have given unto them the words which thou gavest me; and they have received them, and have known surely that I came out from thee, and they have believed that thou didst send me. I pray for them: I pray not for the world, but for them which thou hast

given me; for they are thine. And all mine are thine, and thine are mine; and I am glorified in them.

And now I am no more in the world, but these are in the world, and I come to thee. Holy Father, keep through thine own name those whom thou hast given me, that they may be one, as we are. While I was with them in the world, I kept them in thy name: those that thou gavest me I have kept, and none of them is lost, but the son of perdition; that the scripture might be fulfilled. And now come I to thee; and these things I speak in the world, that they might have my joy fulfilled in themselves. I have given them thy word; and the world hath hated them, because they are not of the world, even as I am not of the world. I pray not that thou shouldest take them out of the world, but that thou shouldest keep them from the evil. They are not of the world, even as I am not of the world.

Sanctify them through thy truth: thy word is truth. As thou hast sent me into the world, even so have I also sent them into the world. And for their sakes I sanctify myself, that they also might be sanctified through the truth".

Jesus prayed seriously and sincerely for His disciples. He acknowledged that God gave them to Him, and He verified that they have been faithful and righteous in verses 6 through 9. We must not overlook the fact that Jesus had an awesome relationship with His disciples. That's why He prayed for them so intensely. In verses 10 through 14, His relationship with them is identified as He makes statements such as: "all mine are thine," "keep through thine own name those whom thou hast given me," "Those that thou gavest me I have kept," and "That they might have my joy fulfilled in themselves." Jesus called the disciples His. He walked with them, taught them, reprimanded them, loved them, and called them to follow Him. The relationship He had with them was very strong because there was constant communication.

Verses 15 through 19 reveal the specifics of Jesus' prayer for His disciples. He prayed for them not to be taken out of the world but to be kept from evil and sanctified through the Word of truth.

Jesus certainly prayed systematically, spontaneously, specifically, and seriously for Himself and for others. Jesus' communication with His Father kept Him disciplined in His work

Last, but not least, Jesus prayed for all believers in verses 20 through 26. Verse 20 says, "Neither pray I for these alone, but for them also which shall believe on me through their word."

Jesus prayed for all those who would receive Him. He prayed specifically for:

⚓ Their oneness in Him
⚓ Their perfection (completion) in Him
⚓ Them to love others with His love

This is the awesome prayer of our Savior. How does our prayer life compare to His? If you will notice, He talked to His Father as if He was face to face with Him. He talked intimately and confidently about all things.

If our relationship with God has grown stale, remember that He is right where we left Him. You too can talk face to face with Him.

List what you have learned about your prayer life from the prayer of Jesus.

According to the prayer of Jesus, what are we to pray for in the lives of those we love?

Find three more prayers of Jesus, and record where they're found in Scripture below.

_____

_____

What is the difference in the prayers of the Pharisee and the publican in Luke 18:9–14?

_____

_____

_____

What type of relationship did the Pharisee have with God?

_____

_____

_____

What one word best describes the publican's heart?

_____

_____

_____

Which one of these men best reflects your current prayer habits?

_____

_____

A New Desire

If you want to have a new desire for Jesus, study Colossians 1:9–14 for yourself. Record anything that you've learned from the passage below.

_____

_____

_____

_____

_____

Daily Journal

Record what you have learned about God and
about yourself from today's lesson.

_____

_____

_____

_____

_____

_____

_____

_____

_____

Solidifying the Partnership

The Love of God

Weekly Thought

Solidify means "to make or become solid; figuratively, to unite firmly."[1] "Partnership means the condition of being a partner or partners; joint interest ; a company or a firm with two or more members who share the risks and profits; a player on the same team; a contract that creates such a relation."[2]

Receiving Christ into our hearts is the only thing that solidifies our partnership with the Holy Savior. Once we do this, our partnership is eternally solid and sealed by the precious blood of the Lamb.

First Peter 1:18–19 says, "for as much as ye know that ye were not redeemed with corruptible things, as silver and gold from your vain conversation received by tradition from your fathers; But with the precious blood of Christ, as of a lamb without blemish and without spot."

---

1 Webster's Pocket Dictionary And Thesaurus Of The English Language, New Revised Edition. (Allied Publishing Group, Inc., of Nichols Publishing Group 1999), p 226

2 Webster, p. 188

A partnership requires much and sometimes gives little in return. Any partnership has both profits and losses. However, we determine the relationship's success or failure according to our personal interest and the amount of time we put into the partnership.

A relationship must be established before a partnership can be formed. Salvation by grace through faith forms the relationship on which we base our collaboration with Christ.

God revealed His interest in and love for us when He gave His only begotten Son. God's love for us and our love for Him are the ingredients that solidify the partnership and establish the depth of the relationship. However, I've seen that our definition of love is sometimes entirely different than God's. The partnership is weakened through our own insecurities. God's definition of love is the one we must abide by to have a solid partnership with Christ Jesus.

What is love? For most of us, it is a four-letter word used loosely to get what we want and to justify our behavior of jealousy, envy, and strife. How many times have we justified our improper behavior by saying, "I reacted like this because I love you so much"? We blame much of our ill behavior on love, but First Corinthians 13 tells us that love is not *puffed up*.

Man's definition of love has always been based on merit, social standing, and personal profit. Man's love is conditional and limited. We measure our love for others according to what they do for us. If they please us a lot, then we love them a lot. If they seem inattentive and distant, then we don't regard them as much. They are not as beneficial to us. Therefore, we tend to avoid them. These facts are sad, but they are so true. We have all been guilty of this at one time or another.

Our love for God is pretty much based on this same system. The more God does for us, the more we do for Him. Our walk with God is based on how good we think He is to us. Our love for Him is just like our love for one another; it is conditional and limited. But the paltry evidence of our love does not reflect the fullness of God's love.

God's love is evident in the giving of His only begotten Son. He gave Him up to death for us. This is why First John 4:10 says, "Herein is love, not that we loved God, but that he loved us, and sent his Son to be the propitiation for our sins." What greater evidence of love is there to be seen? Jesus' love toward us is shown in how He freely gave His life to die for our sins. He loved us so much that He took our place at Calvary. We should take a hard look at our love for Him.

Jesus' example of partnership requires three things from all who believe. These three things are vital for solidifying a profitable partnership in God's kingdom work. They are

- ⚓ responsibility,
- ⚓ reverence, and
- ⚓ respect.

Before we can be partners with anyone, there must first be a willingness to work together as a team. Both parties must have a willingness to share the profit and the loss. As partners with Christ, we are exhorted in Second Timothy 1:8: "Be not thou therefore ashamed of the testimony of our Lord, nor of me his prisoner: but be thou partaker of the afflictions of the gospel according to the power of God."

Responsibility in partnership requires us to endure in times of testing. As the Scripture just stated, there will be times when we must partake of these afflictions. However, how we handle affliction will be the evidence of our level of maturity and responsibility. If we bow out every time we are tested, then we are not very responsible Christians. If we are easily influenced, tempted, and persuaded by the enemy and the world, then our partnership with Christ is very shallow and weak. Second Timothy 2:3 says, "Thou therefore endure hardness, as a good soldier of Jesus Christ." Being responsible partners with our Savior forces us into a life filled with sacrifice, sufferings, and service.

Once we become responsible, we are then challenged with the issue of respect. Regardless of our position, in the partnership there must be respect for the one in authority. Jesus is that one in authority in our partnership with Him, and He deserves all of our respect. He gave His life for us when we showed absolutely no love or respect for Him at all.

Jesus has the controlling interest in this firm of life. He bought us with the price of His life. While we were yet sinners, Christ died for us. Therefore, we must respect not only His person but also His Word and His holiness. As partners with Him, we should be as He is, do as

He does, and love as He loves. Respect is something that is earned, and Christ certainly earned our respect when He took our place at Calvary.

Once we fulfill our responsibility to live for and serve God with utmost respect, then we will be in complete reverence to God and His righteousness. We will fear His authority—not in wrath but in complete adoration of Who He is. We will join Him in service because we long to lift Him up in all we do. We will reverence Him as God of our lives, and we will humble ourselves under His power and in His presence. The greatest asset of being in partnership with Christ is the fact that we dwell in the unconditional love of God. His love holds no boundaries and can never be cancelled. God's love is solid, and we should strive to solidify our love for Him so we can be pleasing partners to our heavenly Father.

There are many examples throughout the Bible of men and women who had solid partnerships with God. Esther's partnership with God stands out above the rest. Enslaved in Persia and reared under the leadership of her cousin Mordecai, Esther was instructed to hide the fact that she was a Jewess. She was chosen by King Ahasuerus to be queen. However, Haman, one of the king's captains, plotted to pass a decree of death that would eliminate all Jews. Mordecai learned of the plot and sent word to his cousin, Esther, who was the king's concubine. He instructed her to go before the king and make an appeal to spare the Jews.

Esther was unsure of her position with the king because she had not been called to come in to the king for thirty days. Esther 4:11 says:

> "All the king's servants, and the people of the king's provinces, do know, that whosoever, whether man or woman, shall come unto the king into the inner court, who is not called, there is one law of his to put him to death, except such to whom the king shall hold out the golden scepter, that he may live: but I have not been called to come in unto the king these thirty days."

Esther reveals to us the one person with whom she knew she had a solid partnership when she sent word to Mordecai for all the Jews to fast for three days and three nights. Esther was acknowledging through this fast that *only God* could work this one out. She may have been uncertain about her partnership with King Ahasuerus, but she knew that God was always there and waiting to hear from her.

Esther's fasting and courage got God's attention, and she became the link to freedom for the Jews. Her partnership with God was so solid that she reveals her responsibility, reverence, and respect when she says in Esther 4:16, "So will I go in unto the King, and if I perish, I perish." Esther was very secure in her partnership with and her love for God.

Partnerships must be secure before they can be profitable. Therefore, it is essential that we understand the love of God so we can excel in a new desire for our Savior.

Day 1: God's Love Defined

First John 4:7–8 says, "Beloved, let us love one another: for love is of God; and every one that loveth is born of God, and knoweth God. He that loveth not knoweth not God; for God is love."

We in the flesh put so many boundaries on love that we fail to make love unconditional and eternal. I am so thankful that God doesn't react in this way toward us.

Love is of God. In order to love, we must have God within us. The evidence of our love is manifested in our position with Him. If we are born again, then we have God's love to give. As His children, we have power to love anyone. We have power to love our enemies and to forgive any wrong done to us.

God's love in us is our power for all things.

God's love is so merciful and forgiving. Every time we activate forgiveness, concern, or comfort toward someone else, we are experiencing God. God is all the love any person needs for all of life's circumstances.

Every time we find ourselves harboring hatred, bitterness, and anger, remember that these things are not of God. God's love can change our heart, and you too can love like He loves. Empty yourself in God's love today. Be willing to release your hatred, bitterness, and anger into God's presence.

In many ways, love has lost meaning in this modern world. We need to remind ourselves of the true definition of love. Where did our parents and grandparents get their definition of love? The pure, sincere love our parents and grandparents knew was learned from God's Word. What is God's definition of love, and from where did it come? John tells us very plainly in the Scripture above, "Love is of God."

Without God in our lives, we have no love. Many of us know people who are unsaved, yet they seem to have love in them. We often mistake affection, infatuation, and the lusts of our flesh for true love, but my friend, make no mistake about it: until you have received Jesus Christ as your Savior, you cannot know true love. God's love can make the most loving person you know more loving, for he or she will experience a new love that he or she has never known before. Inviting Jesus into a rocky marriage can give a marriage that has fallen apart a new love to stand on. Someone who has received God's love into his or her heart through Jesus Christ can love people he or she never thought possible.

This is because true love is found only in Jesus. Through His true love, you can experience new heights of peace and contentment that you never thought existed.

Second Corinthians 13:11 says, "Finally, brethren, farewell. Be perfect, be of good comfort, be of one mind, live in peace; and the God of love and peace shall be with you." Let's get back to the true meaning of love and learn to live in God's peace.

According to First John 4:7–8, how are we taught to exemplify God's love?

_____

_____

_____

_____

_____

_____

Thus far we have learned that God's love gives us power over three things. List them below.

_____

_____

Are you harboring any of the feelings represented by the words listed below? If so, indicate by underlining.

- ⚓ Hatred
- ⚓ Bitterness
- ⚓ Anger
- ⚓ Unforgiveness
- ⚓ Jealousy
- ⚓ Envy
- ⚓ Strife

How does Second Corinthians 13:11 tell us to experience God's love?

Love truly is of God, and it is forever unconditional, but we must remember that we have an enemy. Satan likes to deceive us into thinking that God's love is like our own fleshly love for one another. Satan focuses our attention on our past sins, recurring sins, and destructive habits that seem to control our lives. He uses these things against us to make us feel we are beyond forgiveness and worthless to ourselves, to others, and to God. Then he offers us alternatives that will eventually draw us back out into a sinful world. The result is spiritual defeat and self-destruction.

Satan couldn't care less about us. His intentions are to turn us from God. Satan can't offer us love. He only offers things and relationships that appear to be love, but that eventually end in destruction.

God's love, on the other hand, is real. It is unconditional and nondestructive.

Jesus revealed this love on the Cross. He loved those who crucified Him, asking the Father to forgive them for what they were doing even as they did it! Jesus knew His death would be the atonement for His tormentors. God loved them in spite of their behavior.

God's love is often revealed through His chastening. When the correction is past, we can look back and see that God was not punishing us but loving us. What we view as punishment and hardship is often simply God's love in action.

How can God love a drug addict, an adulterer, a drunk, or a murderer? He does it just like He loves His only-begotten Son, just like He loved David when he committed murder and adultery, and just like He loved Judas Iscariot, who betrayed the Lord for thirty pieces of silver. God's love is a merciful love. Psalm 106:1 says, "Praise ye the LORD. O give thanks unto the LORD; for he is good: for his mercy endureth for ever."

A New Desire

If you want to have a new desire for Jesus, study Romans 8:31–39 for yourself. Record what you learn below.

Daily Journal

Record what you have learned about God and
about yourself from today's lesson.

_____

_____

_____

_____

_____

_____

_____

_____

_____

_____

Day 2: God's Love Developed

For I am persuaded, that neither death, nor life, nor angels, nor principalities, nor powers, nor things present, nor things to come, Nor height, nor depth, nor any other creature, shall be able to separate us from the love of God, which is in Christ Jesus our Lord.

—Romans 8:38–39

Once again we see God's eternal partnership with His children in this passage of Scripture. Absolutely nothing can separate us from His love. There is no greater love than that. Just imagine God loving us in our sin, our disobedience, and our rebellion. He loves us when we reject Him, choosing the world over His righteousness. Wow, what a love!

It is now our responsibility, and should be our passion, to develop this same love in our lives. We develop this love by loving not only ourselves the way God does but also by loving others with His eternal love. This is very hard for most of us. Where do we start? How do we begin to love like God loves?

How can we overcome the hindrances of our flesh and love others in the same way God loves them? First, we must get ourselves into God's Word to learn of Him and His ways. Then we must prayerfully seek to become more like Him. We will find that the closer we get to God, the more like Him we become. God's love is not based on feelings or performances. God's love is a decision. Once we make the decision to love with God's love, nothing will be able to stop or separate that.

We can overcome the flesh by looking at every person and every circumstance through the eyes of God.

We must learn to deal with our feelings and emotions through the power of the Holy Spirit within rather than reacting instinctively in our fleshly nature. Overcoming the flesh requires sacrificing our own thoughts to put on the mind of Christ. We must deny our fleshly desires to be what God wants us to be.

Most importantly, to love with God's love, we must obey the two greatest commandments. We find these commandments in Matthew 22:37–39: "And He said to him, '"YOU SHALL LOVE THE LORD YOUR GOD WITH ALL YOUR HEART, AND WITH ALL YOUR SOUL, AND WITH ALL YOUR MIND." This is the great and foremost commandment. The second is like it, "YOU SHALL LOVE YOUR NEIGHBOR AS YOURSELF"'" (NASB).[3]

Do you love others with God's love? If not, set aside the flesh and get in His Word. Allow God to transform you into a vessel of His love.

How long has it been since you have really studied God's Word?

_____

_____

What more do you feel you could do to develop God's love?

_____

_____

Study Matthew 22:37–39. Record the differences between the heart, the soul, and the mind.

_____

_____

_____

Today we see brokenhearted people everywhere. The news reports are of murder, war, and violence across the nation and around the world. Sin abounds, and in a desperate fight to survive, hearts cry out

---

3   New American Standard Bible. (La Habra, CA: The , 1960, 1962, 1963, 1968, 1971, 1972, 1973, 1975, 1995 by The Lockman Foundation)

for help. Confessions are being made of mistakes, sins, and times of failure.

People are beginning to feel too unworthy to serve our risen Lord and Savior because of their pasts or perhaps even because of some current situation in their lives.

We must realize that God's love for us far exceeds all of our circumstances.

God knows so much more about us than we will ever know about ourselves or others.

God knew Peter more than Peter knew himself. John 21:15–17 shows us that Peter realized this. Having denied the Lord, just as the Lord told him he would, Peter felt like a failure, unworthy of God's love. Yet after the Lord's resurrection, the Bible records this conversation between Peter and the Lord:

> "So when they had dined, Jesus saith to Simon Peter, Simon, son of Jonas, lovest thou me more than these? He saith unto him, Yea, Lord; thou knowest that I love thee. He saith unto him, Feed my lambs. He saith to him again the second time, Simon, son of Jonas, lovest thou me? He saith unto him, Yea, Lord; thou knowest that I love thee. He saith unto him, Feed my sheep. He saith unto him the third time, Simon, son of Jonas, lovest thou me? Peter was grieved because he said unto him the third time, Lovest thou me? And he said unto him, Lord, thou knowest all things; thou knowest that I love thee. Jesus saith unto him, Feed my sheep."

Oh, what a great God we serve! Jesus didn't ask Peter to confess that he had denied Him three times. All Jesus wanted was Peter's confessions of love for Him. He knows the battles and unworthiness we face daily, and His desire is for us to confess our love for and dependence on Him throughout them.

Jesus knew the only way Peter would ever fully develop God's love within Him would be for Peter to get past his failures and teach others.

That's why Jesus told Peter to feed His sheep. When God's love is developed within us, we will then have a desire to partake in our loving partnership with God. God loves us in spite of our rejection and denial toward Him. That's why Jesus said in Luke 23:34, "Father, forgive them; for they know not what they do." I wrote the following poem, entitled "God Still Loves Me" after my own "Peter" experience.

God Still Loves Me

God's love is like a rapid river,
Rushing out of control.
Not even the largest rocks or reefs
Can stop its constant flow.
I know that when I dam His love
With walls of rejection and pain
God loves me still, through it all,
That fact will never change.
He loves me when I hate myself,
And when others could not care less.
God loves me in my weakest hour,
Even when I fail His tests.
So even though I've failed His tests,
One thing from them I've learned;
God still loves me, no matter what,
And His love doesn't have to be earned.

John 3:16–17 says, "For God so loved the world, that he gave his only begotten Son, that whosoever believeth in him should not perish, but have everlasting life. For God sent not his Son into the world to condemn the world; but that the world through him might be saved."

Take time today to thank God for His unconditional love. List your Peter experience below.

_____

_____

_____

Did this experience draw you closer to God, or did the enemy defeat you in it?

_____

_____

List your most recent "failures" below.

_____

_____

_____

What lessons have you learned from the failures listed above?

_____

_____

_____

_____

_____

A New Desire

Find within the four Gospels two more of Peter's experiences and record what you learned from Peter.

_____

_____

_____

_____

_____

_____

_____

Daily Journal

Study the life of Jesus, and record some of His techniques for developing His Father's love within Himself. Then list what you learned from it.

_____

_____

_____

_____

_____

_____

_____

_____

Day 3: God's Love Demonstrated

If, as Scripture teaches, *love is of God* and *God is love* and His love is manifested through His children, then it is safe to say that we are the vessels through whom His love is demonstrated. First John 4:12 tells us how to demonstrate outwardly the love of God within us. It says, "No man hath seen God at any time. If we love one another, God dwelleth in us, and his love is perfected in us."

If you want to demonstrate true characteristics of God's love, you can challenge yourself to obtain the gems of love listed below.

- ⚓ **Limitless:** God's love is limitless and life giving. He loves the drunkard and the murderer just as much as He loves the saint. His love is light as it reflects hope and kindness, and it makes us lively in Him. Our liveliness stems from our knowledge of His almighty presence within us.

- ⚓ **Omnipotent:** God is all-powerful, and His love is omnipotent. This means that the power of God's love can heal the deepest hurt, forgive the greatest sin, and build bridges that only His love can build. When we let God's omnipotent love control our lives, we will forgive when we don't want to forgive. We will love those we don't want to love.

- ⚓ **Valuable:** God's love also makes us valuable to the Lord. As a matter of fact, we were so valuable to God that He gave Jesus for our sins. In God's eyes, we are precious and worth paying for—with the price of His Son's life. I pray that you will recognize your worth as a child of God. You are very valuable to His Kingdom work.

- ⚓ **Eternal:** God's love for us is eternal. He will never stop loving us. We never need to fear the day that God says, "My love for you ends today." *Eternal* means time with no end. Can you say you possess this eternal love for others? Ask God for it!

God's love is truly limitless (no boundaries), omnipotent (all-powerful), valuable, and eternal in all our lives—now and for all time.

Are you harboring a hurt that is preventing you from being a demonstration of God's love? If yes, name the hurt below.

_____

_____

How may this particular hurt be affecting your partnership with God?

_____

_____

Circle the revelation of God's character that you need more of in your understanding of love:

His limitlessness

His omnipotence

My sense of value to Him

His promise of eternal fidelity

Sometimes we wonder if the love within our hearts is truly God's love. We can know this by testing ourselves for the marks of God's love. These marks are found in First Corinthians 13:4–8.

Verse 4 says, "Love suffereth long ..." In other words, true love—God's love—is not quick to resent. True love "is kind ..." The Greek form of the word kind means to be useful. True love will be distributed to others. It is not going to sit inside a person and not be effective.

Next, true love "envieth not." True love isn't jealous over another's good fortune. It "vaunteth not itself ..." True love doesn't lift itself up with praise. It "is not puffed up ..." It does not dwell in pride. Love "doth not behave itself unseemly." This means that love is always exercised in decency and self-control. Love "seeketh not her own."

Those who have the marks of God's love within will seek to edify others over self.

True love "is not easily provoked, thinketh no evil."

True love is enduring and righteous.

It "rejoiceth not in iniquity, but rejoiceth in the truth." Any person who thrives off of gossip, lies, and confusion rather than the truth is less likely to be a person who truly possesses God's love within.

Do your actions toward others hold any of these values? These are the marks of God's love within. If your actions toward others reflect these characteristics of love, then you are allowing God to love others through you. If your actions toward others do not hold true to these values, you are either hindering God's love from shining through you or you do not have God's love within. Examine yourself, and seek God's Word for counsel.

Jesus fulfilled every one of the characteristics of God's love we just studied. His love is always demonstrated with great compassion. The shortest verse in the Bible, which reveals His compassion, states that "Jesus wept" at the death of Lazarus. He wept also for the grief of Mary and Martha at the loss of their brother.

Compassion is definitely one of the characteristics of Jesus Christ. Jesus wept at the loss of a loved one. He understood the desperate attempt of the woman with the issue of blood who was determined to touch His garment. He lovingly faced Peter after Peter had denied Him three times. Most of all, He had compassion as He hung on the cross of Calvary, dying for the sins of a world that hated Him.

Compassionate love is all of this and nothing less. We can't compromise it, and we can't water it down. Compassion runs from deep within the heart, and it stems from an unlimited love. Compassion means to feel sorry for someone. Jesus certainly felt sorry for us as He went to the cross. He had so much compassion for us that He took our place.

First Peter 3:8 says, "Finally, be ye all of one mind, having compassion one of another, love as brethren, be pitiful, be courteous." We must care about other people and the lives they are living. We must show them compassion by helping and praying for them. We can never do someone good by judging him or her. Let God do the judging, and let us show him or her compassion. It is time that we, as Christians, have sympathy toward and feel sorry for one another and for this lost and dying world.

Compassion can be demonstrated
by the smallest of things.

A simple prayer, a short phone call, or a brief visit to someone can brighten his or her day. Perhaps you could send someone a card with words of encouragement or even a bouquet of flowers just to let him or her know that you were thinking about them. Any simple gesture made out of a sincere love for the person you're dealing with is an act of compassionate love.

Have you shown compassion to someone today?

_____

_____

List below your personal definition of the word compassion.

_____

_____

Explain how compassion was shown in Luke 10:30–37.

_____

_____

_____

_____

A New Desire

If you want to have a new desire for Jesus, study Second John 4: 13–21 for yourself. Record what you learn below.

_____

_____

_____

_____

_____

_____

_____

Daily Journal

Record what you have learned about God and
about yourself from today's lesson.

_____

_____

_____

_____

_____

_____

_____

_____

_____

Day 4: God's Love Distributed

When we purpose in our hearts to distribute love, we must give of ourselves—not only to God but also to others. In our partnership with God, He commands us to love our neighbor as we love ourselves.

God distributed His love to us through the cross of Calvary as His only begotten Son took our place and paid our sin debt. The Bible says in John 15:13, "Greater love hath no man than this that a man lay down his life for his friends."

Giving God's love to those who are unsaved, hurting, and hopeless is a responsibility for all of God's people. If we do not distribute the love of Jesus, then how can we expect His love to be manifested? We are God's vessels for distributing love so we must be willing to reach out to others from the depth or our hearts. How do we do that effectively? There are three recommendations that will work if you will apply them:

- ⚓ Love from your heart.
- ⚓ Look for the positive.
- ⚓ Love unconditionally.

Let's study these three recommendations to determine if we are effectively distributing our heavenly Father's love.

Love from Your Heart

The joyous life of a Spirit-filled Christian is described in the text of Ephesians 5:19. This is how we should appear as Christians every day. It says you and I should be "speaking to yourselves in psalms and hymns and spiritual songs, singing and making melody in your heart to the Lord." Notice that the Scripture tells us to do these things in our hearts. When we find our security in the Lord, we can perform these joyous acts even when times seem tough. We can even share the joy of

Jesus with others by giving them a kind and sincere word or a special touch that reflects Christ's love.

When we make melody in our hearts to the Lord, we are in a constant state of praise. We are abiding in Christ, and as a natural result of this state, we spread His love abroad. Do we abide in this state enough that others can see God through our love? We, as Christians, hold that responsibility. We should allow our hearts to reach out and uplift someone each day, whether we feel like it or not.

Jesus has such a loving heart for all mankind. He is no respecter of persons. We are all equal in the eyes of God; every man, woman, boy, and girl is the same. God is proud of each one of us because we are His through Jesus Christ. God knows us and loves us, and it thrills His heart when He sees us helping others along the way.

Jesus is always love, joy, and peace, and we have His character living in our hearts through the Holy Spirit. Submit yourself to sharing the love of your heart with someone today and every day. You are only giving others Jesus, and everyone needs Him. Be joyful! Be happy! Sometimes that's all the love someone else needs.

Name two people you know who need the love of God manifested in their lives right now.

List one thing you could do that would represent God's love in their lives.

Is your partnership with God solid enough that you would willingly do your part as God's vessel in the lives of the two people you listed above?

Look for the Positive

It is important to realize what it takes to have a positive Christian love toward others. First Corinthians 13:7–8 says charity "beareth all things, believeth all things, hopeth all things, endureth all things. Charity never faileth: but whether there be prophecies, they shall fail; whether there be tongues, they shall cease; whether there be knowledge, it shall vanish away." This can only mean that godly love overlooks the worst and continues to love unconditionally.

This is the standard of a positive Christian love. If we can give others the benefit of the doubt rather than having a critical or negative attitude, we can become positive influences in the lives of others. We will become positive Christians expressing positive Christian love.

The only way to be sure we have a positive Christian love is to examine ourselves once again.

If your love is anything other than what has been defined here and in the preceding pages, seek God's Word for counsel. First John 4:16–17 says, "And we have known and believed the love that God hath to us. God is love; and he that dwelleth in love dwelleth in God, and God in him. Herein is our love made perfect, that we may have boldness in the day of judgment: because as he is, so are we in this world."

Are you able to love others regardless of their lifestyles? Are you able to love them even when they do things you don't like? Most of all, are they able to see that your concern for them is truly out of deep, godly love for them? The answers lie within our own hearts.

Can you list a current situation in your life in which you are focused on the negative instead of the positive? Confess it on the lines below.

Do you feel in your heart that you can overcome the negativity and manifest God's love in this situation?

When we love others with positive, unconditional love, we magnify God's master plan for us here in this life. According to First Corinthians 13:7–8, positive Christian love does five things. List them below.

_____

_____

_____

_____

_____

Love Unconditionally

God's unconditional love is the door to the joy of God's love. This is exemplified for us in Luke 15:7. It says, "I say unto you, that likewise joy shall be in heaven over one sinner that repenteth, more than over ninety and nine just persons, which need no repentance." Because love's joy is in seeing sinners saved, this joy can only be found in God's unconditional love. God's love doesn't end when we feel like we have disappointed or shamed Him. When Jesus hung on the cross, He took disappointment and shame with Him. We mistake our own disappointment with ourselves for God's. We let our viewpoints blind us from seeing God's mercy. When we can't love ourselves, we must remember that God loved us so much that He gave His Son so we might have life more abundantly. If God can forgive you, then you must also forgive yourself. God loves and forgives others, and He expects us to do the same.

The drunkest drunk, the most addicted drug addict, the most well-known adulterer, and even the meanest murderer are all valuable to God. He still loves them to the point of changing their lives into the likeness of His Son if they will only believe. God loves the sinner just as much as He loves the saint.

Don't be so quick to condemn others. Be willing to overlook their faults and reach out to their needs. We should be able to love others regardless of our differences with them. Challenge yourself to have the same love toward yourself and others that Jesus had when He said, "Father, forgive them; for they know not what they do." Open the door to love's joy by loving others with God's unconditional love.

Before we can love others unconditionally, we must learn to love God unconditionally. Most of us put limitations on our relationship with God, disrupting the partnership. If God doesn't perform in our lives the way we expect, then we reject and pull away from Him. We accuse Him of letting us down. We accuse Him of not doing His part.

Unconditional love has nothing to do with favor and fulfilled expectations. If this were true, then we would never be able to receive the love of God. We have never done God any favors, and we have never fulfilled any expectations for Him. God has never expected anything from us. Jesus, His Son, fulfilled every expectation of God the Father because He knew we never could. That, my friend, is truly unconditional love.

Is your partnership with God solid? If you love and serve Him without limitations, then you can boldly answer yes to this question. If not, what would it take to get there?

_____

_____

_____

_____

_____

Who in your life do you love with limitations? List those limitations.

_____

_____

_____

_____

What does the Bible teach us about unconditional love in First John 4:20–21?

_____

_____

_____

_____

_____

A New Desire

If you want to experience a new desire for Jesus, study John 21:15–25. Record what you learn below.

_____

_____

_____

_____

_____

Daily Journal

List five ways that we as Christians can distribute God's love. Record what you learned about God and about yourself in these five things.

_____

_____

_____

_____

_____

_____

_____

Day 5: God's Love Described

For the last four days, we have come to understand the definition, development, demonstration, and distribution of God's love. Therefore, today we must challenge ourselves to understand and describe the love of God. Indeed, there is only one word that can describe such unconditional and eternal love: "unfeigned".

What does *unfeigned* mean? Webster defines it as "genuine or sincere."[4] That one common word perfectly describes God's precious, undying love. This love is found in the Bible only twice, and in both Scriptures it urges us to have unfeigned love toward others. Second Corinthians 6:3–6 says,

> "Giving no offence in anything, that the ministry be not blamed: But in all things approving ourselves as the ministers of God, in much patience, in afflictions, in necessities, in distresses, In stripes, in imprisonments, in tumults, in labours, in watchings, in fastings; By pureness, by knowledge, by longsuffering, by kindness, by the Holy Ghost, by love unfeigned."

Regardless of the circumstances around us, we are to prove ourselves godly by demonstrating sincere love. God is love; He is the author and giver of love.

Love is the key to life.

Jesus tells us, in Matthew 22:37–40, "Thou shalt love the Lord thy God with all thy heart, and with all thy soul, and with all thy mind. This is the first and great commandment. And the second is like unto it, Thou shalt love thy neighbour as thyself. On these two commandments hang all the law and the prophets."

Jesus loved us enough to give His life for us. Therefore, His example

---

4   Strong, James, LL.D, S.T.D., The New Strong's Exhaustive Concordance Of The Bible. (Nashville, TN: Thomas Nelson Publishers, 1990), p. 1132, Gk. 505, p. 9

of unfeigned love is the example we should follow as we live each day. Jesus didn't die just for the wealthy or some other special group of people. He died for everyone; His love is for everyone. Jesus loves the sinners just as much as He loves the saints. He even loves those who deny, mock, and abuse Him. He never rejects anyone who comes to Him. This is an unfeigned love.

The unfeigned love of God was demonstrated once again after Jesus' resurrection. The young man in the sepulcher gave the women the message that Jesus had risen, and he told them to go tell the disciples and Peter that He would see them in Galilee (Mark 16:4–7). When He spoke the words, "and Peter," he demonstrated forgiveness and unfeigned love.

Peter's denial did not kill God's love.

Peter had to be tested and taught by the Lord about genuine love, and God will also test and teach us about this love. We often place conditions on our love for others. Therefore, God has to teach us in *His way* how to unconditionally love others.

Unfeigned love is God's love, and we are given the responsibility of seeking and serving others with His love. We can be the greatest Christians in the world, but if we don't show love to others, then our Christianity is null and void in the eyes of God. Paul expounds on the importance of serving and living in love in First Corinthians 13. Throughout the whole chapter, we find that love is the method for everything we do. Verses 4 through 7 say, "Charity suffereth long, and is kind; charity envieth not; charity vaunteth not itself, is not puffed up, Doth not behave itself unseemly, seeketh not her own, is not easily provoked, thinketh no evil; Rejoiceth not in iniquity, but rejoiceth in the truth; Beareth all things, believeth all things, hopeth all things, endureth all things." When we read this, we should not be surprised at the fact that most of our actions of love are just the opposite of Paul's definition of genuine love.

The bottom line is this: when we love others through our flesh, we present a love that is the opposite of that defined by Paul. When we love others with God's love, then we love through our hearts. We see and demonstrate love in the way Paul describes it in the Scripture text. This is the kind of love Jesus demonstrated to Peter when He forgave and forgot Peter's denial.

Are you being tested like Peter? If yes, record the test below.

_____

_____

What do you think God is trying to teach you through this test?

_____

_____

Are others able to see God's unfeigned love in you in spite of your test?

_____

_____

_____

_____

We are always looking for love. Whether it be from our spouses, our parents, our families, our friends, or strangers, we long for love.

*Everyone needs comfort,
encouragement, or a simple smile.*

Many people stop at nothing to find this love; some even turn to drugs, alcohol, and other sinful avenues searching for it. We must reach out to them and offer them God's love by sincerely helping them change their lives.

We do this by teaching them about Jesus, who is the source of all genuine love.

As the source of genuine love, Jesus demonstrated to us the nine principles of love. These principles are given to us in First Corinthians 13. Love is patient, or as Paul says, it "suffers long." Love is kind.

Love is approving, or "envieth not." Love is sharing and "seeketh not her own." Love is calm and "is not easily provoked," and love is righteousness ("thinketh no evil"). This is the kind of love Jesus unselfishly displayed for us on the cross of Calvary even while we were demonstrating the ten things that love is not. What are these?

Love is not envy. James 3:16 says, "For where envying and strife is, there is confusion and every evil work." Love is not arrogant or as Paul says in First Corinthians 13, "puffed up." Love is not selfish; it is not provoked or easily angered, and it is not evil. Love is not unrighteousness, sin, or iniquity. Most of all, love does not fail. All of these things are contrary to the love Jesus demonstrated toward us from Calvary's cross.

Find someone who needs a touch of love, and give him or her Jesus by letting him or her see Him in your life. Love forgives, love heals, love helps, and love is eternal. Won't you give your heart to someone? Jesus gave His heart for you.

List below the ten things that love is not.

_____

_____

_____

_____

_____

Record below any of these ten things you may recognize in your own life. How will you begin to deal with them?

_____

_____

_____

_____

_____

_____

_____

_____

_____

_____

_____

_____

_____

A New Desire

If you want to have a new desire for Jesus, study Matthew 22:37–40 for
yourself. Record what you learn below.

_____

_____

_____

_____

_____

Daily Journal

Record what you have learned about God and
about yourself from today's lesson.

_____

_____

_____

_____

_____

_____

_____

_____

_____

_____

_____

Demonstrating Discipleship

Living in God's Will

Weekly Thought

isciple means a "pupil or follower, a learner, someone who adheres to a teacher's faith." [1] *Discipleship* means, "the state of being a disciple, to understand the teacher and to follow his/her principles and guidelines." [2]

Jesus taught the pure truth of life as He walked and lived among the people in Bible days. He was the teacher of eternal life and righteousness. He still is that teacher, and He is the Way, the Truth, and the Life. His principles and guidelines are to be adhered to today just as they were in Bible days. Luke 14:27 says, "And whosoever doth not bear his cross, and come after me, cannot be my disciple.

As we are challenged to take up our cross, we are challenged to literally die to self. We must crucify the flesh and become as Christ in word, deed, and action, with all of our hearts, souls, and minds.

1   Tenney, Merrill C., Steven Barabas, Th.D., Peter DeVisser., eds. The Zondervan Pictorial Bible Dictionary. (Grand Rapids, Michigan: Regency Reference Library of Zondervan Publishing House, 1963, 1964, 1967) p. 217

2   Barnhart, Clarence L., Barnhart, Robert, eds., The World Book Dictionary.(Chicago, London, Sydney, Toronto: World Book, Inc., 1988), p. 597

Discipleship is a state of intimacy with Jesus Christ. The only way to become a disciple is to be a believer in the death, burial, and resurrection of God's only-begotten Son. Jesus manifested His Father's holiness as He came to earth, took on the form of man, and bore the cross for the sins of the world. Jesus demonstrated discipleship for us when He became obedient to death as He completed His Father's will. God needed a perfect sacrifice, and Jesus willingly fulfilled His Father's plan.

Jesus was a pupil of God the Father, and He had a sincere desire to please Him. He listened to the instructions of God and followed the guidelines and principles set forth for the redemption of mankind. Jesus said in John 5:19–20, "Verily, verily, I say unto you, The Son can do nothing of himself, but what he seeth the Father do: for what things soever he doeth, these also doeth the Son likewise. For the Father loveth the Son, and showeth him all things that himself doeth: and he will show him greater works than these, that ye may marvel."

Just as Jesus' greatest teacher was His Father, so our greatest example, teacher, and leader for true discipleship is Jesus our Savior. Jesus demonstrated effective discipleship by applying five things:

- ⚓ obedience
- ⚓ faithfulness
- ⚓ perseverance
- ⚓ humility
- ⚓ service

When we live our lives for Christ in obedience, faithfulness, perseverance, humility, and service, then we are not only demonstrating discipleship, but we are also fully living in God's will. First Thessalonians 4:1–4 says:

> "Furthermore then we beseech you, brethren, and exhort you by the Lord Jesus, that as ye have received of us how ye ought to walk and to please God, so ye would abound more and more. For ye know what commandments we gave you by the Lord Jesus. For this is the will of God, even your sanctification, that ye

should abstain from fornication: That every one of you should know how to possess his vessel in sanctification and honour."

This passage confirms our responsibility to become disciples of holiness when it calls us to sanctification. To live as Jesus lived is to live a holy lifestyle. Jesus is obedience, faithfulness, perseverance, humility, and service personified. Anytime we are demonstrating these traits in our own lives, we are demonstrating the power and person of Jesus Christ within us. Before we can demonstrate these five traits, we must become pupils, followers, and learners. We must adhere to the instructions of the Teacher.

In Luke 9:22–26, we find Jesus telling the disciples of His upcoming death and resurrection. He said:

> "The Son of man must suffer many things, and be rejected of the elders and chief priests and scribes, and be slain, and be raised the third day. And he said to them all, If any man will come after me, let him deny himself, and take up his cross daily, and follow me. For whosoever will save his life shall lose it: but whosoever will lose his life for my sake, the same shall save it. For what is a man advantaged, if he gain the whole world, and lose himself, or be cast away? For whosoever shall be ashamed of me and of my words, of him shall the Son of man be ashamed, when he shall come in his own glory, and in his Father's, and of the holy angels."

Jesus' intentions were not to impress His disciples by boasting of what He would endure. His purpose was to teach them the principles of becoming dedicated disciples.

It is difficult to understand how such unpleasant methods can generate true discipleship in us. Why must we suffer, be rejected, and even be slain just to prove our profession of faith? This is often easy for a new convert to understand. The excitement of our new life in Christ makes it easy to endure almost anything. However, when the excitement wears off, defeat often comes. It seems that our prayers go unheard and that God has forgotten all about us. In this time of weakness, Satan seeks to devour us before we grow any closer to the Lord.

Perhaps you've faced some battles through the years in your work for the Lord. Feelings of defeat may have caused you to quit in your service for the Lord. Maybe you've decided you'd rather be a bench warmer than take the chance of being hurt or disappointed again.

In the Garden of Gethsemane, Jesus probably felt much the same way, but He didn't give up. Instead of giving in to His feelings or emotions, He gave in to God's will. Jesus taught His disciples the secret to such dedication in the three simple steps to discipleship that we'll study for the next few days: following, fighting, and serving faithfully.

Day 1: Obedience

When children are young, they often have a hard time understanding that someone will always have authority over them. Have your children ever told you that when they grow up, they'll get to be their own bosses? Most children do, and unfortunately many of us, even as adults, have this misconception.

There is always a higher authority. Even for those who are self-employed, we are not our own bosses. We all have to answer to God for our actions at work, at play, and in life. When we recognize His authority in our lives, our responsibility is to put ourselves in subjection to Him, subordinate ourselves to His power, and submit to His leadership. This is the cure for spiritual affliction, for "if God be for us, who can be against us" (Rom. 8:31)?

Obedience requires us to submit to authority; it means to conform to God's righteousness. Acts 5:29 says, "We ought to obey God rather than men." Then, in verse 32, it says, "And we are his witnesses of these things; and so is also the Holy Ghost, whom God hath given to them that obey him." In this particular text, Peter and the apostles were demonstrating obedience to righteousness at a time when compromise would have been easier. In their time of persecution, they remained under complete subjection, subordination, and submission to God's will for their lives. Let's study each of these elements so we can better understand God's will in obedience.

Subjection

Subjection is best understood as putting ourselves under someone else's authority. Karen, my former personal assistant, had a great and simple example of subjection. She described it like this: "It's like being at work. If the boss is not around, we tend to get a little slack, whereas when he is around we strive to be our best." We put ourselves under subjection to him with hopes of impressing the one who has authority over us.

What is the ultimate authority in our life? We often allow ourselves to be controlled by Satan ... or our own self-will. We deceive ourselves into believing that God can't see us because we can't see Him. This type of thought pattern leads to spiritual decline because it prevents us from total subjection to God. We, like our children, don't like the thought of being controlled by someone else. Eventually, this determination to rule our own lives rather than subjecting ourselves to God's authority will lead to trouble and heartache. Giving in to self-will causes us to end up in subjection to Satan.

Satan tempts our self-will through the lust of the flesh, the lust of the eyes, and the pride of life (First John 2:16). Giving in to any of these is like falling into a trap. What we think is only a small matter of self-indulgence ends up as spiritual warfare with Satan. Romans 13:1 says, "Let every soul be subject unto the higher powers. For there is no power but of God: the powers that be are ordained of God." Sincerely applying these words to our hearts will protect us from the traps set by Satan.

> *Total subjection to God is the first key to*
> *obedience and spiritual victory.*

Total subjection means believing on Jesus unto salvation, giving ourselves obediently and completely to His service, and acknowledging His power and authority in our life by confessing Him in every step, move, and breath we take. Jesus is the power in our life for everything we face. Philippians 4:13 says, "I can do all things through Christ which strengtheneth me."

Subordination

When we are becoming obedient, Christ-minded Christians who can overcome spiritual afflictions, subordination goes hand in hand with subjection.

Luke 7:6–8 gives us a beautiful picture of subordination. In verse eight, the centurion sends a message to Jesus saying,

"For I also am a man set under authority, having under me soldiers, and I say unto one, Go, and he goeth; and to another, Come, and he cometh; and to my servant, Do this, and he doeth it." Centurions were Roman military officers. Although generally disliked because of their harshness and domination, this particular centurion's humility and faith stood out to Jesus. This man of authority sent the message to Jesus that, as powerful as he was, he felt unworthy for the Lord to personally approach him. He humbled himself by saying, "Lord, trouble not thyself: for I am not worthy that thou shouldest enter under my roof: Wherefore neither thought I myself worthy to come unto thee: but say in a word, and my servant shall be healed."

> *We have access to all the promises of God if*
> *we are willing to be under His authority.*

Jesus Himself said in John 14:13–14, "And whatsoever ye shall ask in my name, that will I do, that the Father may be glorified in the Son. If ye shall ask any thing in my name, I will do it." Psalm 10:4 says, "The wicked, through the pride of his countenance, will not seek after God: God is not in all his thoughts." Lay aside your pride, and humbly submit your authority to the Lord, just as the centurion did.

Subordination to God will demand the laying aside of self-control. Too often we disobey God because we want to be the one in control. The centurion was a man with authority and control, but when the Lord's power and presence were active, the centurion heeded to them. His subordination put him in obedience to God.

Submission

Once we've learned to live in subjection and subordination to God's will, we must then learn to submit to it.

> *To be in submission to God means, "surrendering*
> *our all to Him",* [3] *literally giving ourselves*
> *and everything we have to Him.*

---

3   Strong, James, LL.D, S.T.D., The New Strong's Exhaustive Concordance Of The Bible. (Nashville, TN: Thomas Nelson Publishers). P. 1022, Gk. 5293, p.94

It also means that we are walking in total obedience to His will for our lives. If we surrender ourselves and become obedient to God, then being controlled by God and under His authority automatically becomes a part of our daily walk.

Salvation is the gift God freely gave to us; we should give submission in return. Submission requires sacrifice. God has blessed us with everything we have, but He wants us to use it all for His honor and glory. If things in our lives hinder us from submitting to God's will, we should realize this and be willing to let them go. Revelation 3:17 says, "Because thou sayest, I am rich, and increased with goods, and have need of nothing; and knowest not that thou art wretched, and miserable, and poor, and blind, and naked." Our worldly possessions are no good unless they are used for God.

Submitting self to God is often easier than submitting our possessions to Him, but God can't have control if we are not willing to give Him all. Jesus submitted Himself to God, willingly and obediently going to the cross for our sins. Don't become so entangled in possessions that you forget your need for God. What is more valuable than the price He paid for you? Surely nothing.

If you are not in obedience to God in subjection, submission, and subordination, then you are not living fully in His will. If you have lost your desire for growth or if you can't feel God's presence, then it's very possible you are denying God's will to pursue your own.

We must deny self. We must be willing to lay aside our wants and needs for the sake of Jesus Christ. This is true discipleship. Jesus denied Himself for our needs. His self-denial can be seen throughout His earthly ministry. When Jesus prayed, "Not my will, but thine, be done," He laid aside even His life for our sins.

Obedience also requires us to sacrifice our time and pleasures to spend quality time with the Lord and in His service. Jesus spent endless days and nights teaching that obedience required forsaking all to follow Him. Matthew 8:19–20 says, "And a certain scribe came, and said unto him, Master, I will follow thee whithersoever thou goest. And Jesus saith unto him, The foxes have holes, and the birds of the air have nests; but the Son of man hath not where to lay his head." Our Lord gave up His heavenly abode with His Father to dwell among man without even a place to lay down for rest. Jesus explained to the scribe that the decision to follow Him would require many sacrifices.

Submission is the final key to following Jesus. Submission forms a relationship between Christ and us. In other words, we must submit ourselves to a state of obedience to Christ. First Corinthians 11:3 says that Christ is the head of every man.

Do you feel you are walking in total obedience to God? Why or why not?

To follow God more perfectly in obedience, do you need to become more:

⚓ subjective
⚓ subordinate
⚓ submissive

Go back and review the definitions of subjection, subordination, and submission.

Write down the definition for the one you need more of below. Find a passage of Scripture relating to the one you need. Study this passage, and record below what you've learned.

On a scale of one to ten, with ten being the most effective, how would you rate your effectiveness in demonstrating discipleship according to your level of obedience? Circle your answer?

1   2   3   4   5   6   7   8   9   10

On this same scale, where would you like yourself to be? (What is your goal level?)

1   2   3   4   5   6   7   8   9   10

A New Desire

If you want to have a new desire for Jesus, find three people in the Bible who lived in complete obedience to God. List them below.

_____

_____

_____

_____

_____

Daily Journal

Record what you have learned about God and
about yourself from today's lesson.

_____

_____

_____

_____

_____

_____

_____

_____

Day 2: Faithfulness

Most people in this world, even professing Christians, have no concept of who God is, even though their lives are operating and surviving under His mercy and grace. Isn't it a good thing that His mercy is new every morning? Lamentations 3:22–23 reminds us of God's patience in our lives. It says, "It is of the LORD'S mercies that we are not consumed, because his compassions fail not. They are new every morning: great is thy faithfulness."

Many Christians have made a profession of salvation, yet their lives show no reflection of Christ-likeness. They attend the local assembly and show up at special meetings and fellowship activities. However, they're also dabbling in sin, wanting the best of both worlds. They are struggling between what God wants for their lives and what they desire for themselves. These people need to become more faithful to God. God is faithful to love us and provide for us according to His will.

Our problem with being faithful to God surfaces when we reject God's will to fulfill our own desires.

If we were only *half* as faithful to Him as He is to us each day, our lives would be so much easier.

Notice that the verse in Lamentations says, "It is of the Lord's mercies that we are not consumed." God is so faithful to love us with a boundless love. It is His love that extends His mercy to us. In all of our sin, our daily battles of the flesh, and the temptations of the enemy, God's mercy protects us from death and destruction.

We must challenge ourselves to be more faithful to live a life of righteousness. God should be able to say of us as we stand before Him, "Great is thy faithfulness." In what areas of your life do you need to be more faithful? What first step could you take toward that end today?

God's will for your life is for you to be faithful in all things. True discipleship is demonstrated through our consistency to stay true to God and His holiness. Luke 16:10–13 says:

> "He that is faithful in that which is least is faithful also in much: and he that is unjust in the least is unjust also in much. If therefore ye have not been faithful in the unrighteous mammon, who will commit to your trust the true riches? And if ye have not been faithful in that which is another man's, who shall give you that which is your own? No servant can serve two masters: for either he will hate the one, and love the other; or else he will hold to the one, and despise the other. Ye cannot serve God and mammon."

God entrusts us to be ministers of His righteousness. If we are not faithful to Him, then we can expect great trouble in our lives. God holds us responsible in our relationship with Him. He entrusts us with the service of being examples of His love and salvation. As disciples we have responsibilities, and we are to remain faithful to God by fulfilling them. When we are faithful in the small as well as the great, then we can say we are living in God's will. In demonstrating discipleship, we should be faithful to serve Him, share Him, and sacrifice for Him.

Often we come up with excuses for our failure to be all God wants us to be.

"You don't know what is going on in my life right now," we say. It may be true that others can't understand your situation, but God's Word says in Romans 8:35–36, "Who shall separate us from the love of Christ? Shall tribulation, or distress, or persecution, or famine, or nakedness, or peril, or sword? As it is written, For thy sake we are killed all the day long; we are accounted as sheep for the slaughter." This should be a consolation to you, regardless of your circumstances.

The text teaches that we should never allow anything to keep us from being faithful in all God wants us to do. Perhaps you're having financial problems, and you're ashamed to go to church to pray and worship because of this. God has not stopped loving you; He is still there. Maybe you're having marital problems that you're afraid will end in divorce, so you feel you shouldn't serve God publicly due to your situation. Friend, these excuses are not accepted by God. Regardless of your circumstances, God loves you, and He longs for you to be faithful in serving Him in spite of the situation.

Our problem is no excuse for our failure to be all that God wants us to be. Instead, our excuses simply become unfaithfulness. Our situation can't separate us from the love of God. Rather, such tribulations and distresses should provoke us to total dependence upon Him. After all, He is the only one who can deliver us from these circumstances. Romans 8:37 says, "Nay, in all these things we are more than conquerors through him that loved us." Don't defeat yourself in your life for Christ; give Him control, and conquer your circumstances!

Daniel is a great example of a faithful man of God. He refused to worship the false gods of King Nebuchadnezzar when in captivity. He refused to stop praying to the only *true* God. Daniel knew that every refusal to obey man, in order to stay faithful to God would bring suffering, but he still stood true to God's will.

Daniel's faithfulness to God brought him through many things by God's power. You see, God honored Daniel's faithfulness, and God always protected and provided a way of escape for His faithful servant.

It was not always easy for Daniel. He was cast into a lion's den and thrown into prison, and men sought to destroy his life, but God in His faithfulness was always with him. Daniel knew God was worthy of whatever he had to face to remain faithful.

Knowing our responsibilities doesn't make it any easier to fulfill them, but God is worthy of our love, praise, and undivided attention. The joy of fulfilling our responsibilities in Christ is found in Second Corinthians 4:16: "For which cause we faint not; but though our outward man perish, yet the inward man is renewed day by day." Each time we stand for the gospel's sake, we will be renewed, through either suffering or rich harvest, with the strength of God through the Holy Spirit.

We must not allow the lust of our flesh to take precedence over our responsibilities before God. Hebrews 12:6 tells us that there is a price to pay for this. "For whom the Lord loveth he chasteneth, and scourgeth every son whom he receiveth." We must also be cautious against the snares of the devil. Our adversary will give us many alternatives to fulfilling our responsibilities. Satan takes our wants, desires, and weaknesses and uses them to distract us from serving God, and he's very subtle about doing it. Second Corinthians 11:3 says, "But I fear, lest by any means, as the serpent beguiled Eve through his subtlety, so your minds should be corrupted from the simplicity that is in Christ." First Peter 5:8 says, "Be sober, be vigilant; because your adversary the devil, as a roaring lion walketh about, seeking whom he may devour." God can protect us from the enemy and show us how to overcome the desires of our flesh so we can fulfill our responsibilities with joy.

Jesus faithfully and willingly fulfilled His responsibility as He hung on the cross. Let's become responsible Christians, and let's honor our Lord and Savior each day by serving Him no matter what the cost. Psalms 101:6 says, "Mine eyes shall be upon the faithful of the land, that they may dwell with me: he that walketh in a perfect way, he shall serve me."

Are you faithful in demonstrating discipleship?

Can you list here three things you have been faithful in?

What is one thing that you know prevents you from being more faithful to God?

List one persecution you experienced because you chose to stay faithful to God.

A New Desire

From whom did that persecution come?

- ☐ family
- ☐ friend
- ☐ stranger
- ☐ fellow Christian
- ☐ other

A New Desire

If you want to have a new desire for Jesus, study the life of Elijah, in First Kings 17:1–18 and 41–46. Record Elijah's faithfulness below.

_____

_____

_____

_____

_____

Daily Journal

Record what you have learned about God and
about yourself from today's lesson.

_____

_____

_____

_____

_____

_____

Day 3: Perseverance

Perseverance means, "steadfastness and persistence." [4] God's will for our lives is that we persevere in our relationship with Him. Persevering means that we endure through the hard times when we have absolutely no strength to endure.

Our relationship with God will be tested. However, our obedience and faithfulness will be demonstrated through our determination to persevere. True discipleship is exemplified when, instead of quitting on God and giving up, we stand in His Word when our Christian character is attacked. Jesus gives us a great example of lack of endurance in the parable of the sower in Mark 4:16–17. It says, "And these are they likewise which are sown on stony ground; who, when they have heard the word, immediately receive it with gladness; And have no root in themselves, and so endure but for a time: afterward, when affliction or persecution ariseth for the word's sake, immediately they are offended."

Righteousness calls for us to be strong in the faith, determined to remain steadfast and rooted in the truth of God's Word. Therefore, perseverance is another key principle for demonstrating discipleship, and it is vital for living in the will of God. Jesus defines the process of perseverance in Luke 9:23: "And he said to them all, If any man will come after me, let him deny himself, and take up his cross daily, and follow me." Our Lord bore a literal cross on Calvary, but He also carried a spiritual cross of rejection, persecution, and mockery on each day leading up to Calvary.

The battles we face do not come when we are in a state of sin; our battles come when we are living in righteousness. Jesus said in Luke 12:51, "Suppose ye that I am come to give peace on earth? I tell you, Nay; but rather division." This division is righteousness against unrighteousness. The unrighteousness of the flesh, the world, and Satan are constantly at warfare with the righteousness of the Spirit within us

---

4   Barnhart, Clarence L., Barnhart, Robert, eds., The World Book Dictionary.(Chicago, London, Sydney, Toronto: World Book, Inc., 1988), p. 1554

A New Desire

(Gal. 5:17). Our salvation places us into an eternal position with Christ through which we have power to win any battle. The key to victory is abiding in Christ. John 14:27 says, "Peace I leave with you, my peace I give unto you: not as the world giveth, give I unto you. Let not your heart be troubled, neither let it be afraid."

Every battle won is a step toward a more intimate relationship with God. Each battle lost or given up only sets us back in our spiritual growth. God uses our battles to strengthen us for His ministry. Second Corinthians 12:9 says, "And he said unto me, My grace is sufficient for thee: for my strength is made perfect in weakness."

God uses our weaknesses in the battle to prove His strength.

The battle is His, and the victory is ours. Fight the good fight of faith, and become a dedicated disciple.

Perseverance in righteousness consists of three ingredients:

⚓ conflict
⚓ confidence
⚓ continuance

Conflict

Many Christians are under the impression that life in Christ is full of blue skies, rainbows, wealth, and prosperity. This concept is easily misunderstood because many have never been taught differently. We mistake the happiness that material possessions and worldly success give us for the true joy that is found only in God. It is hard for those who believe this to understand what has happened when problems arise. We see in Philippians 1:29 that the Bible completely contradicts the teaching of "health, wealth, and prosperity." "For unto you it is given in the behalf of Christ, not only to believe on him, but also to suffer for his sake." From Genesis to Revelation we are taught that being Christlike means suffering and conflict. Jesus was "bruised for our iniquities." He faced many conflicts in His ministry each day. He was despised and rejected by the very people whom He died to save.

Romans 5:3–4 gives us hope while enduring the conflicts we face. "And not only so, but we glory in tribulations also: knowing that tribulation worketh patience; And patience, experience; and experience, hope."

> *Jesus endured conflict with the hope of*
> *seeing the world come to repentance.*

Our hope in conflict is both in seeing others come to repentance and in seeing our Lord come again someday soon to call us away from this world of conflict.

Conflict in our lives is a sign of one of two things. Either we are distant from God and He is trying to get our attention or we are in the center of His will and growing and learning from our experiences. Sometimes it's hard to understand, but God will not put more on us than we can bear.

Describe your most pressing present conflict below.

....

....

Is this conflict brought on by your living for God or by your degree of distance from Him?

....

....

....

In what way has this conflict affected your confidence in pursuing God?

....

....

A New Desire

Confidence

Despite the conflicts we face as Christians, we can have confidence in our victory over them through Jesus Christ. His death, burial, and resurrection give us confidence for every area of our lives because He has given us victory even over death, hell, and the grave.

Our confidence can be increased through studying God's Word. His Word is our assurance of victory through all of life's trials.

Hebrews 13:5–6 says, "Let your conversation be without covetousness; and be content with such things as ye have: for he hath said, I will never leave thee, nor forsake thee. So that we may boldly say, The Lord is my helper, and I will not fear what man shall do unto me."

Confidence in life requires contentment in life.

That is the principle taught in these verses.

We must learn to be content with what God has given us and where He has placed us. If we try to do things outside of God's will or ahead of Him, we set ourselves up for spiritual warfare. When we try to walk independently, we place our confidence in ourselves and in our fellow man. We leave God completely out of the picture, and when our plans fail, we lose confidence in Him. However, there is no reason for lack of confidence in God. Instead, we must learn to trust in Him completely.

Jesus gave His life for us; we should learn to trust Him for all of our needs. When we learn to trust Him in all things, we will find that even our conflicts increase our confidence in Him, for even in conflict He is working out His will in our lives. We can overcome conflict by "Being confident of this very thing, that he which hath begun a good work in you will perform it until the day of Jesus Christ" (Phil. 1:6).

How does your lack of confidence affect your ability to demonstrate discipleship?

Check the box for each area in which you presently lack confidence.

⚓ Your knowledge of God's Word
⚓ Your salvation experience
⚓ Your abilities
⚓ Your availability
⚓ Your reputation as a Christian
⚓ Your stability
⚓ Your love for God

Ephesians 3:16–20 contradicts our lack of confidence in the things listed above.

⚓ In verse 16, what are we granted?
⚓ In verse 17, what are we to be?
⚓ In verse 18, what are we able to do?
⚓ In verse 19, what are we filled with?
⚓ In verse 20, what is God able to do?

Right now, at this point in time, are you willing to continue in your discipleship journey? What does the next step appear to be?

_____

_____

Continuance

Confidence that we can overcome the conflict we face gives us the strength to continue on in our journey. Paul understood that conflict was necessary, that victory was guaranteed, and that there was a reason to continue on in spite of it all. Paul said in Philippians 1:12, "But I would ye should understand, brethren, that the things which happened unto me have fallen out rather unto the furtherance of the gospel." Paul knew that the conflicts and victories in his life were all for the purpose of spreading the gospel in some way.

Are you continuing on in your work for the Lord, or have you quit on God because things became more than you thought you could bear? Paul came to a point where he too wanted to quit. In Philippians 1:21–24 he said, "For to me to live is Christ, and to die is gain. But if I live in the flesh, this is the fruit of my labour: yet what I shall choose I wot not. For I am in a strait betwixt two, having a desire to depart, and to be with Christ; which is far better: Nevertheless to abide in the flesh is more needful for you." Paul knew that leaving behind the troubles of this world and being in the presence of the Lord would be better for him, but for the sake of others and the furtherance of the gospel, he chose to continue on in his work for the Lord. Paul's love for the people at Philippi was greater than his weakness of suffering in the flesh.

Our greatest example of continuance is found in Jesus Christ.

Jesus died, rose on the third day, and then ascended into heaven, where He sits at the Father's right hand, making intercession for us. What if He had left one of these undone? Where would we be today?

Be joyful in the Lord, and continue in His service! *Persevere*— regardless of what life dishes out, refuse to be defeated!

A new desire for Jesus is activated in our heart each time we make it through the battle. There are sure to be battle scars, but isn't it better to have scars that signify victory and perseverance in Jesus rather than wounds of defeat?

In Matthew 4:8–9, what did Satan use to challenge Jesus' perseverance in righteousness?

What was Jesus' response to Satan's proposition in Matthew 4:10?

What choice was Satan left with in Jesus' determination to persevere?

In Matthew 4:11, how was Jesus rewarded for His perseverance?

....

....

Perseverance is a choice. We can either walk away from God in
the heat of the battle or we can trust Him to carry us through. Which
choice have you made and why?

....

....

....

A New Desire

Find in the Bible (both Old and New Testaments) someone who
demonstrated conflict, confidence, and continuance in his or her
relationship with God. List what you learned from this person that
you can now apply to your own life.

....

....

....

....

....

Daily Journal

Record what you have learned about God and
about yourself from today's lesson.

Day 4: Humility

John 3:30 best exemplifies the definition and process of humility. It says, "He must increase, but I must decrease." This is humility plain and simple. When we decrease, God is able to perform His will through us. "The word decrease means to lessen (in rank or influence), to make lower."[5] Humbling ourselves means the same thing. In other words, we must recognize God's greatness and our own smallness.

Humility was the dominant characteristic of Christ as He so freely gave His life for us. Philippians 2:8 says, "And being found in fashion as a man, he humbled himself, and became obedient unto death, even the death of the cross." He literally took our place at Calvary so we might receive Him unto salvation and magnify Him. This is why we should apply First Peter 5:6 to our lives. It says, "Humble yourselves therefore under the mighty hand of God, that he may exalt you in due time."

Humility is the key to becoming pleasing to God. Until we can put ourselves into a life of meekness and lowliness, God will never be able to use us in His service. There is no way to effectively demonstrate obedience, faithfulness, and perseverance until we have clothed ourselves with humility. First Peter 5:5 says, "Yea, all of you be subject one to another, and be clothed with humility: for God resisteth the proud, and giveth grace to the humble."

God does resist the proud because the proud put themselves before and above God. The proud have no use for God; they think they can do all things without Him. The proud also refuse to help others because they can't see another person's need. All they can see is their faults.

Humility demands a willingness to bear another's burdens and to realize that this life is about leading others to a relationship with Jesus instead of focusing on self. We have no power to help others without God abiding in us. John 15:5 says, "I am the vine, ye are the branches: He that abideth in me, and I in him, the same bringeth forth much

---

5   Strong, James, LL.D, S.T.D., The New Strong's Exhaustive Concordance Of The Bible. (Nashville, TN: Thomas Nelson Publishers, 1990), p. 256, Gk. 1641, p.29

fruit: for without me ye can do nothing." We will begin to experience God's holiness in our lives once we realize we are nothing without Him. We will keep to ourselves the things we once boasted about, knowing that God is pleased with us and that's all that matters.

Humility is evident when people fulfill these things:

- They put God first.
- They think of others above themselves.
- They acknowledge that they can do nothing without God.
- They focus on others' needs above their own.
- They realize God's greatness and their smallness.
- They have a burden for the lost.
- They see themselves as God's vessel.
- They hunger for righteousness.
- They totally depend on God.
- They exemplify self-denial.

You see, humility is about giving God the glory for all things. Jesus said that the works He did were the works of His Father. He uplifted His Father instead of Himself, and now our responsibility is to uplift Jesus. We have the Holy Spirit's power to do that. God's divine will for our lives is for us to humble ourselves before the Lord so He can draw the lost to Himself. John 12:32 says, "And I, if I be lifted up from the earth, will draw all men unto me." The greatest reward for any of us is to see men drawn to God through our lives of humility. We must come to God in sincerity, confessing our sin and allowing Him to rule our lives. We must give Him complete authority over our hearts, minds, and souls. Jesus gives a beautiful example of humility in Matthew 18:1–5. It says:

> "At the same time came the disciples unto Jesus, saying, Who is the greatest in the kingdom of heaven? And Jesus called a little child unto him, and set him in the midst of them, And said, Verily I say unto you, Except ye be converted, and become as little children, ye shall not enter into the kingdom of heaven.

Whosoever therefore shall humble himself as this little child, the same is greatest in the kingdom of heaven. And whoso shall receive one such little child in my name receiveth me."

A little child is innocent, dependent, and teachable in the eyes of God. We too must approach Him with such humility. Do you demonstrate humility in your pursuit of discipleship?

_____

_____

Can you list your latest demonstration of humility?

_____

_____

How did Moses demonstrate humility in Exodus 3:11?

_____

_____

In Jeremiah 1:6, humility is demonstrated by Jeremiah's realization that he was as what?

_____

_____

_____

What was the name of the woman who demonstrated humility in Luke 1:43 when she said, "And whence is this to me, that the mother of my Lord should come to me?"

_____

_____

_____

_____

Humility is not an option in your relationship with God. You must come humbly before Him, giving yourself wholly to His will. God honors your humility, and He is faithful to use your humility for His service. Proverbs 22:4 defines the reward for our humility. It says, "By humility and the fear of the LORD are riches, and honour, and life."

A New Desire

If you want to have a new desire for Jesus, list the areas in your life you need to become more humble in. Then, ask God to humble you.

_____

_____

_____

_____

Daily Journal

Record what you have learned about God and
about yourself from today's lesson.

_____

_____

_____

_____

_____

_____

_____

Day 5: Service

For the last four days, we have individually studied the elements that are necessary for being in God's will and for demonstrating discipleship. Thus far we have been taught obedience, faithfulness, perseverance, and humility. The final element can be none other than our service as children of God.

God's divine will for all born-again believers is for them to serve Him. Not only are we to serve with joy and gladness, but we should also serve with a zeal and desire to see lost souls saved and the hurting given hope and comfort. Our service in righteousness is not only for the lost and dying world; it is also for spiritually young and hungry Christians. We are to be examples for the cold and indifferent as well as to fellow brethren who serve in ministry and the local assembly alongside us. Jesus says this about serving in John 12:26: "If any man serve me, let him follow me; and where I am, there shall also my servant be: if any man serve me, him will my Father honour." The word "honor"[6] in this verse means to prize or to value. Wow! God truly values those who willingly serve Him.

We cannot be disciples of Christ until we are willing to serve. Jesus gives us an example of a faithful servant in Luke 9:24–26:

> "For whosoever will save his life shall lose it: but whosoever will lose his life for my sake, the same shall save it. For what is a man advantaged, if he gain the whole world, and lose himself, or be cast away? For whosoever shall be ashamed of me and of my words, of him shall the Son of man be ashamed, when he shall come in his own glory, and in his Father's, and of the holy angels."

Giving up our lives is the principle of becoming a servant. Giving up our lives is a strong statement, but it is meant to be taken literally.

6   Strong, James, LL.D, S.T.D., The New Strong's Exhaustive Concordance Of The Bible. (Nashville, TN: Thomas Nelson Publishers, 1990), P. 506, Gk. 5091, p. 90

To become servants, we must die to the flesh, giving up our old lives and desires so we can become separated from sin and unrighteousness. We are already dead to sin (Rom. 6:6–11), but we must crucify the flesh and its lusts daily.

Our life is found in God when we become faithful servants.

Now we walk in the Spirit rather than in the flesh, desiring to serve God and others. This is the example that Jesus set for us. He gave up His life to become a servant to sin and death, taking the penalty of sin from us so we could have eternal life. Philippians 2:7 says He "made himself of no reputation, and took upon him the form of a servant, and was made in the likeness of men."

Paul urges us to take upon ourselves the same type of humble service as Jesus did. Philippians 2:5 says, "Let this mind be in you, which also was in Christ Jesus." In order to take on the mind of Christ and become faithful servants, we must come humbly, willingly, and ready to live an unhindered, dedicated Christian life.

How can we know whether we are in God's will? The key to finding the answer lies in First John 3:22, which says, "Keep his commandments, and do those things that are pleasing in his sight."

How can we know God's commandments and what is pleasing in His sight? Study the life of Christ. Seek to know His personality and the intentions of His actions. Seek to comprehend His motives for everything He said and did. Each book of the Bible, from the Old Testament to the New, presents Christ's purposes and personality in some form. There is nothing about the life of Christ we can't find out about if we will but study the Word of God.

If we want to keep God's commandments and do the things that are pleasing in His sight, we must be like Jesus. We must seek Him and listen to His counsel. We must know what He requires of us and trust Him for guidance. God's Word is our only sure way of knowing if we're in God's will. The counsel of others, the fleeces we put out, and our gut feelings can deceive and mislead us, but God gave us the Word of God to guide our steps. The Bible encourages us to seek the counsel of others, but we must stay true to the Word of God above all else.

God's Word lays down three requirements for being in God's will. First, we must be born again. Second, we must depend totally upon God. Anything that is not of faith does not please God (Rom. 14:23). Finally, we must be willing to serve Him. We must be willing to live for Jesus if we are ever to know we are in His divine will. If we are fulfilling these three requirements, we are pleasing to the Father. Therefore, we are in His will.

Can we be in Christian service outside of God's will? Keep in mind what we've learned thus far. Hebrews 11:6 says that Satan seeks to devour those who are unsure about their service for the Lord. Often we take a job in the church just because someone asks us to, and we never seek the Lord for His direction. This can cause us to lose our peace and joy in service. How can we be sure our service is in God's will?

Pray and seek God, and then listen attentively for His voice. God's will often requires sacrifice.

Therefore, we must be sure that we are rooted and grounded in God's Word. When our service calls for sacrifice, Satan will be on hand to remind us of what we're giving up. Be sure we are secure enough in God's Word that we are able to stand against the wiles of the devil.

If we are uncertain about God's will for our service, take some time to slow down and listen for His voice. Ask Him to reassure you about what you're doing and whether it is pleasing in His sight. If you still can't find peace, perhaps it's time to take greater measures. If necessary, seek God through fasting and prayer until you've positively heard from Him. Fasting may be a challenge for you, but sometimes we must lay aside our flesh for the cleansing of our souls. Remember, First John 5:14 assures us that God will reveal His will to us when it says, "And this is the confidence that we have in him, that, if we ask any thing according to his will, he heareth us."

There is no limit to what we can do or be for the Lord if it is according to His will for our lives. Don't limit God and His power with unbelief! So many times we accept salvation freely, but we don't want to serve God wholeheartedly. We even try to tell the Lord what we can and can't do for Him according to our own lifestyles. In this way, we limit God's power in our lives. Rather than letting God lead us into service for Him, we tell *Him* what we're comfortable with doing.

A great example of limiting our service for the Lord is found in Mark 10:17–22. This is the story of the rich young ruler who wanted eternal life—until he found out what he had to do to get it. The rich young ruler didn't understand that he had been asked to give up all he had. Jesus told him to give it to the poor so he would have treasures in heaven. He couldn't understand that giving up the temporal things of the world would give him eternal things that hold so much more value. His unwillingness caused him to go away from Jesus grieved and empty-handed.

We are much like the rich young ruler. We want the benefits of Christianity, but we don't want to sacrifice for them. We don't want to labor or to repent. We get so caught up and comfortable with the things of this world that we don't want to give them up. This is what causes our service—when it costs us nothing—to lose its value in the eyes of God.

We are what we want to be in our relationship and in our service before God. As the body of Christ, we have as much access to God and His power as we want. Serving God is our choice, so how much of a desire do we have to be His servant?

We can have a servant's heart just like Jesus, but we must crucify the flesh and its lusts so we can serve with liberty. Galatians 4:9 says, "But now, after that ye have known God, or rather are known of God, how turn ye again to the weak and beggarly elements, whereunto ye desire again to be in bondage?"

Based on the life of Christ, there are a number of requirements for becoming a servant who effectively demonstrates true discipleship. These requirements were not only demonstrated by Christ, but they were also applied by the twelve who were chosen by Jesus, excluding Judas Iscariot. We too must apply these to our lives to become servants of righteousness.

In my study of the eleven faithful disciples, I have matched each of their names with the characteristic that best fit their service. Who would you relate to most in your life of discipleship service?

1. Steadfast—Peter (He was the *rock* on which Christ built His church.)
2. Faithful—Andrew (He was always wherever Jesus was.)
3. Dedicated—James, the Son of Zebedee
4. Devoted—John, the brother of James
5. Anointed—Philip (He was a soul winner.)
6. Obedient—Bartholomew, called Nathanael
7. Repentant—Thomas, also called Didymus
8. Humble—Matthew, the publican (or tax collector)
9. Peculiar—James, the Son of Alphaeus
10. Follower—Thaddaeus
11. Zealous—Simon the Canaanite

Obedience, faithfulness, perseverance, humility, and service are the five main things Jesus Himself demonstrated as He fulfilled His Father's will. Which of these do you already possess? List them below.

Name the ones you feel you lack, and record your studies of each below.

What is in your past, present, or future that is hindering you from being a servant of righteousness?

A New Desire

If you want to have a new desire to live for Jesus, study the spiritual gifts. Record below which gifts you have and how God would have you use them in His service.

_____

_____

_____

_____

_____

Daily Journal

Record what you have learned about God and
about yourself from today's lesson.

_____

_____

_____

_____

_____

_____

_____

_____

Refining the Fellowship

The Power of Forgiveness

Weekly Thought

To *fellowship*, means, "to participate, to distribute; companionship, the state or condition of being one of a group."[1]

Refine, or refining, means, "to purify, to become free from impurities."[2]

Once we solidify our position as one of God's children, we not only possess salvation, but we also have fellowship with Him. Salvation makes us part of the bride of Christ.

The depth of fellowship we have with Christ is based upon our faithfulness to live a life of holiness. This refining takes place as we realize and confess our impurities and turn to God for the power to become free of them. Forgiveness provides access to eternal life and develops an intimate fellowship with Jesus Christ. First Corinthians 1:9

1   Strong, James, LL.D, S.T.D., The New Strong's Exhaustive Concordance Of The Bible. (Nashville, TN: Thomas Nelson Publishers, 1990), P.355, Gk. 2842, p. 50

2   Webster's Pocket Dictionary And Thesaurus Of The English Language, New Revised Edition. (Allied Publishing Group, Inc., of Nichols Publishing Group 1999) P.207

says, "God is faithful, by whom ye were called unto the fellowship of his Son Jesus Christ our Lord."

Refining the fellowship is not usually taught in our local assemblies and religious organizations, yet it is of utmost importance in our daily relationship with God. If we are seeking to have companionship with God and to become an effective part of His fellowship, then we must free ourselves of the things that break sweet communion with Him. We allow many obstacles, such as sin, worldliness, and most of all forgiveness (or the lack of it) to impair our fellowship with God.

Jesus was the first to demonstrate the power of forgiveness and to pave the way for "whosoever will" to enter into complete intimacy with God. While we were yet sinners, Christ died for the ungodly. He freely gave His life for those who persecuted and rejected Him. I'm talking about you and me; I'm talking about the Jews, the Gentiles, and different religious sects who refuse to heed to the commandments of God when they make their own laws and commandments. Christ began refining (making pure) our fellowship with God long before we wanted anything to do with Him. To this end, God chose us before the foundations of the world. Ephesians 1:3–7 says:

> "Blessed be the God and Father of our Lord Jesus Christ, who hath blessed us with all spiritual blessings in heavenly places in Christ: According as he hath chosen us in him before the foundation of the world, that we should be holy and without blame before him in love: Having predestinated us unto the adoption of children by Jesus Christ to himself, according to the good pleasure of his will, To the praise of the glory of his grace, wherein he hath made us accepted in the beloved. In whom we have redemption through his blood, the forgiveness of sins, according to the riches of his grace."

Notice that verse seven states that "we have redemption through His blood, the forgiveness of sins." Christ's fellowship with us began with redemption and forgiveness. Redemption means that the ransom was paid in full; forgiveness means receiving pardon and remission.

We are refined by redemption through His blood because His blood cleanses us from all our impurities. Once we have applied the blood, our sins are atoned for, and we have forgiveness. We receive full pardon, and God's forgiveness is activated permanently in our lives.

It is God's desire to fellowship with His children. He longs to have His children participate in and distribute the gospel of Jesus Christ. Likewise, our heavenly Father desires for His children to free themselves from any impurities that taint the good news of Jesus.

Jesus Christ freely forgave us. We must also exercise this forgiveness toward others to operate under the guidelines of God's Word and walk in full fellowship with God. Luke 6:37 says, "Judge not, and ye shall not be judged: condemn not, and ye shall not be condemned: forgive, and ye shall be forgiven." Jesus Himself spoke these words. Forgiveness refines the fellowship—not only is it between ourselves and God but also between ourselves and others.

Once we experience the power of forgiveness, we will realize that God's will for our lives is to live a purified life, free from the sin of unforgiveness. As forgiveness is activated, we find ourselves totally consumed with a new desire to live for Jesus. Ephesians 4:31–32 says, "Let all bitterness, and wrath, and anger, and clamour, and evil speaking, be put away from you, with all malice: And be ye kind one to another, tenderhearted, forgiving one another, even as God for Christ's sake hath forgiven you." As we study the power of forgiveness, be prepared for a transformation in your own fellowship with God!

Day 1: The Price of Forgiveness

The word, *crucifixion* is used, "to represent death on a cross." According to Merrill C. Tenney's *Bible Dictionary*, "this was the most cruel and barbarous form of death known to man. It was so dreaded that, even in the Pre-Christian era, the cares and troubles of life were often compared to a cross. Many pass over the reality of the crucifixion by simply stating, 'They crucified Him.' The whole picture is much more brutal. Before the actual ordeal itself, the prisoner was bent over and tied to a post, where a Roman lector would apply blow upon blow to his bare back with a lash intertwined with pieces of bone or steel. This scourging was frequently sufficient to cause death. Another factor of the agony was the painful but nonserious character of the wounds inflicted to accomplish crucifixion itself. There were two distinctive methods of affixing a living victim to a cross—tying or nailing.

It is well established that Christ underwent the horror of the latter, possibly both processes. In it, the slightest movement would be accompanied with additional torture. Hanging for such a long period of time induced traumatic fever. Finally, death by crucifixion came from heart failure." [3] David describes the agony of it in Psalm 22:14: "I am poured out like water, and all my bones are out of joint: my heart is like wax; it is melted in the midst of my bowels." Jesus' heart literally burst and emptied into His stomach.

"Death by crucifixion was usually hastened by the breaking of the legs." [4] With Jesus, this was not necessary because, as the Bible states in John 19:33, "when they came to Jesus, and saw that he was dead already, they brake not his legs." Jesus wasn't killed by these people; He gave up His life. They just tortured Him until He died. Jesus confirms this

---

3   Tenney, Merrill C., Steven Barabas, Th.D., Peter DeVisser., eds. The Zondervan Pictorial Bible Dictionary. (Grand Rapids, Michigan: Regency Reference Library of Zondervan Publishing House, 1963, 1964, 1967), p.189

4   Tenney, Merrill C., Steven Barabas, Th.D., Peter DeVisser., eds. The Zondervan Pictorial Bible Dictionary. (Grand Rapids, Michigan: Regency Reference Library of Zondervan Publishing House, 1963, 1964, 1967), p.189

fact in John 10:17–18. He says, "Therefore doth my Father love me, because I lay down my life, that I might take it again. No man taketh it from me, but I lay it down of myself. I have power to lay it down, and I have power to take it again. This commandment have I received of my Father."

Jesus bore the cross, suffered the crucifixion,
and died for our sins of His own free will.

He chose to willingly die, taking our place to spare us from the pit of hell.

This is the reality of the cross. Without Jesus' death, burial, and resurrection, the reality of hell's fire would already be manifested in our lives. Jesus described the realness of hell for us in Mark 9:43–44. He said, "And if thy hand offend thee, cut it off: it is better for thee to enter into life maimed, than having two hands to go into hell, into the fire that never shall be quenched: Where the worm dieth not, and the fire is not quenched." The reason Jesus used the word worm in these Scriptures is because He knew that to the Jews, fire and worms always represented internal and external pain. He wanted to let us know that hell is a horrible place that is filled with pain, agony, and torture that will never end.

Jesus did not make hell for us. He made hell for Satan and his angels. Matthew 25:41 says, "Then shall he say also unto them on the left hand, Depart from me, ye cursed, into everlasting fire, prepared for the devil and his angels." If we reject Jesus Christ as our personal Savior, then we have made the decision to go to hell; the cross and the Crucifixion are null and void in our lives. Disobedience in accepting Jesus as Savior will cast us into hell fire. The choice is ours alone.

Christ's death on the cross was a horrible one, but He did it just for you. How much more personal could anyone ever get in your life? Do you know of anyone else who would die for your wrongdoings? Hell will be even more horrible for you than the cross was for Jesus. Christ gave up the ghost and died, but in hell the worm dies not. If you refuse Christ's atonement for your sins on earth, you will live eternally in outer darkness in a lake of fire, devoid of God's love. Matthew 8:12 says, "But the children of the kingdom shall be cast out into outer darkness: there shall be weeping and gnashing of teeth."

Have you made a decision in your life about Jesus or Satan, heaven or hell? No one can make this decision for you; Christ has left it up to you alone. All you have to do is confess your sins to God; ask Him to forgive you and to save you. Believe by faith that because you asked Him, He came into your heart, and He now lives within you through His Holy Spirit.

The price of forgiveness was paid for us by Jesus. It is now time for us to show forgiveness by sacrificing our pride and asking those we have hurt to forgive us, humbling ourselves before God as we ask for His forgiveness to be applied to our own hearts.

The price of forgiveness comes with the realization of three things about ourselves:

- ⚓ We are not worthy of God's forgiveness.
- ⚓ We must deny self.
- ⚓ We are not perfect. –but we are forgiven.

God's Word teaches us that while we were sinners, Christ died for the ungodly. That would be *you and me*. His blood is the only thing that has made us worthy of God's forgiveness. The Bible also teaches us that we must decrease and He must increase. This refers to complete self-denial so that Christ can work in us and through us. The book of Romans says there is none righteous and that we have all sinned and come short of the glory of God (Rom. 3:23).

Yes, the price of forgiveness is great, but Jesus paid that price. Aren't you glad it has been paid in full? What you couldn't do, Jesus did for you.

Is your pride in the way of forgiveness?

Prov. 13:10

_____

....

List the areas where you need to break the pride that hinders forgiveness in your life.

_____

_____

_____

What does Proverbs 16:18 say about pride?

_____

_____

_____

_____

A New Desire

If you want to have a new desire to live for Jesus, study Psalm 22 and record below what you learn about God's love for you from this Psalm.

_____

_____

_____

_____

_____

_____

Daily Journal

Record what you have learned about God and
about yourself from today's lesson.

_____

_____

_____

_____

_____

_____

_____

_____

_____

_____

A New Desire

Day 2: Finding Forgiveness

Throughout life we make mistakes, experience failure, harbor the past, and battle childhood experiences. These matters leave us wounded and scarred, and they often lead us into a life of sin. How?

We experience feelings of unforgiveness and unworthiness in our mental and emotional battles. We become sensitive to negative voices, and then we start believing those voices. We find ourselves questioning our worth and God's power to forgive our past, our mistakes, and even our present iniquities. In our search for forgiveness, we often look to man when Jesus is the only source of forgiveness.

No ordinary man can provide forgiveness for our sin. Never has anyone else had the power to grant forgiveness freely to all. Only Jesus, being the Son of God, could bestow upon us such a gift. Romans 5:6–8 says, "For when we were yet without strength, in due time Christ died for the ungodly. For scarcely for a righteous man will one die: yet peradventure for a good man some would even dare to die. But God commendeth his love toward us, in that, while we were yet sinners, Christ died for us."

When Jesus gave Himself on the cross, we found forgiveness. In nine hours of pure torture, Jesus gave His life as a ransom and paid the price for our sin. As unworthy as we are, He forgave and loved us.

Nothing could have stopped the death, burial, and resurrection of Jesus Christ. He was determined to be the final sacrifice for sin. He died for the very ones who crucified and rejected Him. Jesus never held a grudge. He never wanted revenge, and He never hated anyone. The power of His forgiveness is awesome. Nothing can ever separate us from His forgiving love!

David always knew where to find forgiveness in his time of sin. Psalm 130:3–4 says, "If thou shouldest mark iniquities, O Lord, who shall stand? But there is forgiveness with thee, that thou mayest be feared." David knew that finding forgiveness in God would restore his fellowship with God. David knew that man could not heal his sin. God was his fortress and his forgiveness. If he had sought his deliverance from man, David would have lived a defeated life. We too must turn only to God for deliverance. Man does not have the power, the nature, or the heart to bestow divine forgiveness on the lives of others.

Jesus is the one and only holy Lamb of God without spot or blemish. As we look to Him, we find redemption. First John 1:9 says, "If we confess our sins, he is faithful and just to forgive us our sins, and to cleanse us from all unrighteousness."

Finding forgiveness requires confession from the heart. We can ask for forgiveness all day long in hopes of soothing our consciences, but until we search for forgiveness to soothe our hearts and to cleanse our souls, forgiveness will only be a temporary fix in broken fellowship with God.

As we search for true forgiveness, God will honor our sincerity, and refinement will take place. Searching for forgiveness starts the purifying process, and "God is faithful to forgive." In Psalm 25:16–18, David cried out to God in sincerity for deliverance. He said, "Turn thee unto me, and have mercy upon me; for I am desolate and afflicted. The troubles of my heart are enlarged: O bring thou me out of my distresses. Look upon mine affliction and my pain; and forgive all my sins." Through David's plea, God knew his request was from the heart. David made a valid appeal before the only one who had power to forgive him.

It is time that we refine our fellowship with Jesus by looking for forgiveness and finding it at the Cross. It is time we bow in humility, confessing our sin and turning to Him for deliverance and healing. Second Chronicles 7:14 says, "If my people, which are called by my name, shall humble themselves, and pray, and seek my face, and turn from their wicked ways; then will I hear from heaven, and will forgive their sin, and will heal their land."

If you want to find forgiveness for your sins (past, present, and future), then you must abide by the four orders just revealed to us in the above Scripture. We must

⚓ humble ourselves,

⚓ pray,

⚓ seek God's face, and

⚓ turn from our wicked ways.

Are you practicing all four of these? If not, list below the ones you still need to apply.

_____

Is there something in your life (past or present) that you don't feel God has forgiven you for? List it below.

_____

_____

What does Psalm 86:5 teach us God is ready to do?

_____

_____

_____

A New Desire

If you want to have a new desire to live for Jesus, study the crucifixion in Matthew 27–28. Record below what you learn.

_____

_____

_____

_____

_____

Daily Journal

Record what you have learned about God and
about yourself from today's lesson.

_____

_____

_____

_____

_____

_____

_____

_____

Day 3: Receiving Forgiveness

From yesterday's study, we can see that we sometimes look for forgiveness in all the wrong people and places. When we don't find forgiveness, we build walls of rejection and pain. We begin to feel that forgiveness is impossible. This weakness of our minds becomes the battleground for the enemy's lies, and he deceives us into believing God can never forgive our sin.

Colossians 1:12–14 counteracts this lie of the devil and the weakness of our flesh by reminding us that we can receive forgiveness. It says:

> "Giving thanks unto the Father, which hath made us meet to be partakers of the inheritance of the saints in light: Who hath delivered us from the power of darkness, and hath translated us into the kingdom of his dear Son: In whom we have redemption through his blood, even the forgiveness of sins."

This Scripture should be enough to transform our minds and rebuild the hope to go on in our lives. Why doesn't it have the effect on us that it should? Why can't we accept what it says and move on? The answer is simple: We still live in the flesh, and the flesh battles the Spirit every day. For most of us, we are not studied enough or strong enough in the Lord to understand and to accept God's unconditional love. Therefore, we let our flesh control our thoughts and actions. When we do this, we unwittingly reject the new life Christ has bestowed upon us. Why?

The flesh feels unworthy of God's forgiveness. We know that Jesus is our Savior, yet we may be unwilling to accept His forgiveness. We are even unwilling to *forgive ourselves*. This leaves room for Satan to deceive us into believing God would never use someone as sinful and unworthy as we are. Insecurity and inadequacy leave an open door for Satan's deceptions.

We must learn to reject the lies of the devil and accept the forgiveness Jesus offered on Calvary's cross. We have "all sinned and come short of the glory of God." None of us is perfect in this life, but if Jesus is our Savior, we have hope. Jesus lives in our hearts through the Holy Spirit. His blood has washed our sins away, and we are made holy, blameless, and unaccused.

At the cross of Calvary, our old accounts were settled.

Our slates were cleaned. Our sins are remembered no more. We can start over in Jesus, trusting Him for all things.

The blood of Jesus has made us free from the destruction of sin, trials, persecutions, and rejections that we battle daily in this life. In the flesh we face these things, but through our new life in Christ, we have power to deal with and overcome them. The Bible says in John 16:33, "These things I have spoken unto you, that in me ye might have peace. In the world ye shall have tribulation: but be of good cheer; I have overcome the world."

We must simply die to self and lay everything at Jesus' feet. It is time we became the children of God who claim, accept, and demonstrate our new lives in Christ! It is time we let old things pass away and allow God to bless us with the new things life in Him contains.

God doesn't remember our sins and iniquities, so why can't we forget them? He is the one we must answer to, and through Him, we have overcome the world. Through salvation, our old account with Him was settled; therefore, we should settle our old account in our own hearts. Not to do so is to risk standing in disagreement with God, which is not wise!

Once you receive forgiveness, you will no longer be in bondage to yourself and the sins and mistakes you have made. Jesus released you from that bondage when He said, "It is finished."

Be of good cheer. Through Christ, you have overcome the past. Receive God's forgiveness so you can experience *a new desire* for Him.

What is one thing for which you feel you just cannot receive forgiveness? Confess it below.

_____

_____

Is it possible that you are looking for forgiveness from man instead of from God? If yes, list the person from whom you are seeking to receive forgiveness.

_____

_____

_____

Record First John 2:1–2 on the lines below. Record what you have learned about receiving forgiveness from these verses.

_____

_____

_____

_____

A New Desire

If you want to have a new desire to live for Jesus, study the life of Rahab in the second and sixth chapters of Joshua. Record what you learn below.

_____

_____

_____

_____

_____

Daily Journal

Record what you have learned about God and
about yourself from today's lesson.

_____

_____

_____

_____

_____

_____

_____

_____

Day 4: Activating Forgiveness

In Matthew 6, Jesus taught the disciples how to pray. He not only taught them the secret for finding and receiving forgiveness, but He also taught them how to activate forgiveness. In verses 14 and 15, He says, "For if ye forgive men their trespasses, your heavenly Father will also forgive you: But if ye forgive not men their trespasses, neither will your Father forgive your trespasses."

If we refuse to forgive those who have hurt us, then we will not be able to experience God's forgiveness in our own lives. Activating forgiveness in the lives of those who have intentionally and despitefully used us is a representation of God's power upon us.

Forgiving those who have hurt us is hard, even if the hurt was unintentional. We may claim to forgive them, yet can't seem to get past what happened. We experience painful memories, and before we realize it, we have a mass of unforgiveness harbored in our hearts. This puts us in a state of hindered fellowship with God.

When Jesus taught the disciples about effective prayer, He told them to forgive as they had been forgiven. Matthew 6:12 says, "And forgive us our debts, as we forgive our debtors." Jesus taught the disciples that the key to being effective for Him is forgiving all who have hurt us.

Failure to forgive is sin. God wants you to confess your unforgiveness. God is faithful to hear your prayers, but your prayers will not be effective until you forgive others.

Unforgiveness is a poison to the heart.

It destroys any kindness, compassion, or desire we have within our heart to live for God. Is there someone in your life you have not forgiven?

Unforgiveness causes us to seek revenge and retaliate with hatred and viciousness. We find ourselves paranoid about the genuineness of others. The greatest problem with unforgiveness is the bitterness and the wall we build to protect ourselves from any more pain. We end up in self-pity, wondering what we did to deserve such hurt.

In the Old Testament, Joseph is a great example of someone who was used, abused, and hurt. He was one of the twelve sons of Jacob. He was hated by his brothers, thrown into a pit, sold for twenty pieces of silver, falsely accused by a woman, and then thrown into prison. How many more reasons would a person need to have a spirit of unforgiveness? But Joseph did not harbor unforgiveness. He had love in his heart toward his enemies, and he forgave.

Joseph didn't want anything to stand in his way of receiving God's forgiveness. Joseph understood the principle of Matthew 6:15: "If ye forgive not men their trespasses, neither will your Father forgive your trespasses." I pray that you may comprehend the message in this verse. Don't harbor unforgiveness in your heart. Confess and activate forgiveness today so you can receive the power and blessing of God's forgiveness in your life each day as well.

Is there someone in your past whom you have not forgiven?

_____

_____

How often are you reminded of the hurt that person brought upon you?

_____

_____

Does that person know you are harboring unforgiveness toward him or her?

_____

_____

What does Mark 11:25 command us to do?

_____

_____

_____

A New Desire

If you want to have a new desire to live for Jesus, study in depth the life of Joseph as told in the book of Genesis. Record what you learn about forgiveness below.

_____

_____

_____

_____

_____

Daily Journal

Record what you have learned about God and
about yourself from today's lesson.

_____

_____

_____

_____

_____

_____

_____

_____

Day 5: Living Forgiveness

Jesus Christ was and is living forgiveness. He became forgiveness in living form. Isaiah 53:3–7 says:

> "But He [was] wounded for our transgressions, [He was] bruised for our iniquities; The chastisement for our peace [was] upon Him, And by His stripes we are healed. All we like sheep have gone astray; We have turned, every one, to his own way; And the LORD has laid on Him the iniquity of us all. He was oppressed and He was afflicted, Yet He opened not His mouth; He was led as a lamb to the slaughter, And as a sheep before its shearers is silent, So He opened not His mouth (NKJV)."

This is a picture of Jesus on Calvary. Put yourself in His place for a moment. Imagine yourself literally loathed and rejected by those you have devoted your life to: your parents, your children, your companion, your friends, your coworkers, your fellow Christians, and even your dog. Could you hold up under the feelings of rejection? Jesus did!

God knew that we neither could nor would pay sin's price, so He sent His Son, Jesus, the one perfect, sinless man, to die in our place.

By His stripes we are healed. Our sins are forgiven. We have the free gift of salvation. Jesus did it all because He loves us. First John 1:9 says, "If we confess our sins, he is faithful and just to forgive us our sins, and to cleanse us from all unrighteousness." Oh, what a beautiful picture of grace!

Grace is our access to eternal life. Grace comes from Jesus Christ. Grace protects us from a literal hell. We have grace to live and grace to die. Grace is Jesus on the cross with all our sins upon Him. Think about it; every sin you have ever committed was nailed to Calvary's cross!

Christ was the atonement for all sin. First John 1:7 says, "But if we walk in the light, as he is in the light, we have fellowship one with another, and the blood of Jesus Christ his Son cleanseth us from all sin." This, my friend, is the definition of grace. He forgave not only yesterday's sins and today's but tomorrow's and forever's sins as well.

Grace is being able to receive forgiveness without having to pay the price. Jesus paid for it on Calvary. Grace is knowing that you may sin today, hurt someone's feelings, or be rude, selfish, or unloving, and you'll still be loved unconditionally by Christ. Grace is being able to confess such actions and know that God knew about them already; He was waiting, with grace in hand, for you to confess and repent of them.

Grace is knowing that in everything we face, we are not alone. Jesus has already been there, and He's there to help us through it. Hebrews 4:15–16 says, "For we have not an high priest which cannot be touched with the feeling of our infirmities; but was in all points tempted like as we are, yet without sin. Let us therefore come boldly unto the throne of grace, that we may obtain mercy, and find grace to help in time of need."

You too can become living forgiveness. As you live for Christ, you are being conformed to the likeness of His image. Therefore, you have power to forgive others, love others, and manifest Christ's character through your actions and behavior.

We are the vessels of God's forgiveness. We are to extend His forgiveness everywhere we go. Regardless of how many times we are hurt, rejected, and abused, we must forgive. Matthew 18:21–22 says, "Then came Peter to him, and said, Lord, how oft shall my brother sin against me, and I forgive him? till seven times? Jesus saith unto him, I say not unto thee, Until seven times: but, Until seventy times seven."

When we can forgive and forgive and keep on forgiving, we can then say that we are truly living in forgiveness.

Are you living in forgiveness?

Who are you refusing to continuously forgive?

List the problem with the one who is offending you.

What does God say in His Word about the problem above?

A New Desire

If you want to have a new desire to live for Jesus, study God's continued forgiveness toward the nation of Israel. Record what you learn about living forgiveness below.

Daily Journal

Record what you have learned about God and
about yourself from today's lesson.

_____

_____

_____

_____

_____

_____

_____

_____

Wonderful Worship

The Presence of God

Weekly Thought

orship means, "to fawn or crouch, prostrate oneself in homage (do reverence, to adore)"[1]. It means to "*honor*".[12]

John 4:23 says, "But the hour cometh, and now is, when the true worshippers shall worship the Father in spirit and in truth: for the Father seeketh such to worship him."

In that verse, Jesus reveals what should be the Christian's ultimate priority: worship. We should prostrate ourselves at the feet of Jesus in sincere service, thanking and praising Him for our salvation.

The father knows the heart of each person and its level of devotion to Him. He draws those whose hearts are perfect toward Him.

The level of worship for every believer varies according to each person's depth of intimacy with Jesus Christ. The word "worship

---

1   Strong, James, LL.D, S.T.D., The New Strong's Exhaustive Concordance Of The Bible. (Nashville, TN: Thomas . P. 1237 , Gk. 4352, p.76

is often misunderstood yet is very rarely defined in the public assembly of today's worship centers. Let's examine this important word and practice now.

Worship has been misconstrued as an outward ritual of reverence and respect to God in a local assembly that usually happens once or twice each week. However, worship has nothing to do with a tabernacle, and it has no designated time or place. Worship should be experienced daily, everywhere, at all times.

> ### Worship is best understood as something inward that is produced outwardly.

It can't be produced by a building. Worship comes from a living organism that has the Spirit of God dwelling within. No manmade structure can produce the presence of God.

Jesus taught the woman at the well the correct and honorable method of worship in John 4:23–24. He said, "But the hour cometh, and now is, when the true worshippers shall worship the Father in spirit and in truth: for the Father seeketh such to worship him. God is a Spirit: and they that worship him must worship him in spirit and in truth." Jesus revealed both the honorable and dishonorable methods of worship in these key verses.

The woman at the well had been influenced by two means of worship throughout her life. The first was the way her people, the Samaritans, worshiped. The Samaritans had rejected most of the Old Testament, with the exception of some of the books of Moses, so their worship was very limited by ignorance. Samaritan worship was characterized by outward excitement without inward understanding. The Samaritans worshiped in spirit but not in truth. Jesus revealed this in John 4:22 when He said, "Ye worship ye know not what ..." The Samaritans worshiped from deep within, but they worshiped in confusion because of their misunderstanding of truth. *Worshiping in spirit* means worshiping from the heart with good intentions. However, worshiping in spirit is not true worship if it lacks truth.

The Jews worshiped in truth but neglected spirit. They honored all of the Old Testament teachings, but they rejected the spirit. Their worship was based on truth (the Word), but their worship was void of the power of God. They did not show forth the Spirit of God abiding with them. Therefore, their worship (tithing, praying, fasting, serving, etc.) was of no effect. Their worship was in vain. Jesus rebuked this type of worship in Mark 7:6–7. He said, "Well hath Esaias prophesied of you hypocrites, as it is written, This people honoureth me with their lips, but their heart is far from me. Howbeit in vain do they worship me, teaching for doctrines the commandments of men." We can have all the truth we need, but without worship in the Spirit, it is considered hypocrisy and heresy in the eyes of God.

Now we understand that worship is the only way to get God's attention. Worshiping God in Spirit and in truth is the very thing that places us in the presence of the Lord.

Worship goes beyond the public scene at the local worship center. It goes beyond singing and attending church. It starts first in the person with salvation, an activation of faith, and a repentant life. Then praise and sincere service will make your worship public.

Once we understand true worship, our lives will never be the same.

Very few Christians operate under God's guidelines of righteous worship. Now is the time to put ourselves in a state of real worship. The King James Version of the Bible lists the word worship 108 times. For each listing, the definition implies reverence, obedience, and humility before and service to God.

God's command to us on worship is clearly stated in Exodus 34:14. He says, "For thou shalt worship no other god: for the LORD, whose name is Jealous, is a jealous God." Putting God first is true worship. As we do this, we will find ourselves with a renewed desire to truly sit in His presence.

In Exodus 3, Moses stood in the presence of God in the desert of Horeb. The angel of the Lord appeared unto him in a flame of fire out of the midst of a bush. Before Moses could actually approach God, he was commanded to take off his shoes. Exodus 3:4–5 says:

"And when the LORD saw that he turned aside to see, God called unto him out of the midst of the bush, and said, Moses, Moses. And he said, Here am I. And he said, Draw not nigh hither: put off thy shoes from off thy feet, for the place whereon thou standest is holy ground."

It was imperative that Moses remove his shoes for a couple of reasons. First, removing his shoes represented complete reverence to the presence and holiness of God. Then, removing his shoes was a symbol that nothing should come between man and God. Moses's shoes were between his feet and holy ground. Something material and manmade was the only thing separating Moses from being in the total presence of God.

If we want to be where Jesus is, if we desire to sit in heavenly places, if we would see a burning bush not consumed by the fire, we too must take off our shoes. We must remove the things that stand between ourselves and God.

Shoes in our Scripture text represent *sandals* or *slippers*. It is a symbol of occupancy. It could also be a latchet. Getting on holy ground requires loosing the latchet, putting off what is preoccupying us. We must take off our shoes of sin, hindrance, negativity, and adversity.

God is saying to us today, "Draw not nigh hither until you have unlatched yourself from the things that come between Me and you." He is saying, "I am here, but you have brought with you things that bind My presence from being revealed."

Hebrews 12:1 says, "Wherefore seeing we also are compassed about with so great a cloud of witnesses, let us lay aside every weight, and the sin which doth so easily beset us, and let us run with patience the race that is set before us." Ephesians 4:31–32 says, "Let all bitterness, and wrath, and anger, and clamour, and evil speaking, be put away from you, with all malice: And be ye kind one to another, tenderhearted, forgiving one another, even as God for Christ's sake hath forgiven you."

Just as God instructed Moses to take off his shoes, we must do the same to come into the presence of God.

Acknowledge and then let go of the things below that may be hindering you from getting on holy ground.

Deception	Hurt	Disappointment	Anger
Grief	Unkindness	Sin	Unforgiveness
Rage	Evil-speaking	Disobedience	Evil
Unworthiness	Complaining	Bitterness	Frustration
Misery	Hatred	Discouragement	Gossip
Greed	Other _____		

Day 1: Worshiping in Spirit

Paul said in Romans 1:9, "For God is my witness, whom I serve with my spirit in the gospel of his Son." The word spirit in this verse refers to the inner person. Worship, then, comes from the inside out. When Paul says, "I serve with my spirit," he's implying that he serves from the depths of his heart. Paul worshiped God with a sincere desire from deep within himself. It was not a shallow, outward, hypocritical type of worship.

> *We cannot truly worship unless we've been born again by receiving Christ as our Savior.*

Worship in spirit requires laying aside the flesh. We will worship more as we feed our flesh less. The Jews are a great example of this. They had knowledge and truth, but they had the wrong spirit for worship. That's why Jesus called them hypocrites; they were boasting in their flesh rather than worshiping in the Spirit of God. They worshiped through manmade rituals, and their worship was not honored by God.

Self is the number one hindrance for true worship in the spirit. This hindrance comes in many common forms, but the end results are always the same. Hindrances prevent us from worshiping in a way that is pleasing to God.

We often find it easy to excuse ourselves from God-honoring worship. We blame our lack of sincere worship on busy schedules, lack of interest, preoccupation, and so on. However, the real problem is defined in one word: *self!* Those who allow excuses for their lack of worship are seeking to satisfy their flesh rather than to magnify the Lord. If we will ever truly worship God in spirit, we must set aside self, selfish wants and needs, and the advantages in life we frequently place above God. To worship God in spirit, we must truly die to self.

Worship in spirit also requires us to be in submission to the Holy Spirit. The Holy Spirit produces true worship in us. As we've already learned, true worship begins with salvation, when the Holy Spirit first indwells the believer. Unless you're saved, you have neither the power nor the ability to worship in the Spirit. Romans 8:1–9 says:

"There is therefore now no condemnation to them which are in Christ Jesus, who walk not after the flesh, but after the Spirit. For the law of the Spirit of life in Christ Jesus hath made me free from the law of sin and death. For what the law could not do, in that it was weak through the flesh, God sending his own Son in the likeness of sinful flesh, and for sin, condemned sin in the flesh: That the righteousness of the law might be fulfilled in us, who walk not after the flesh, but after the Spirit. For they that are after the flesh do mind the things of the flesh; but they that are after the Spirit the things of the Spirit. For to be carnally minded is death; but to be spiritually minded is life and peace. Because the carnal mind is enmity against God: for it is not subject to the law of God, neither indeed can be. So then they that are in the flesh cannot please God. But ye are not in the flesh, but in the Spirit, if so be that the Spirit of God dwell in you. Now if any man have not the Spirit of Christ, he is none of his."

The Spirit of God penetrates our hearts and prompts us to worship sincerely. He pricks our hearts for service as He pierces our inner spirit with a conviction that will produce righteous worship. As He renews our minds in truth, He places our thoughts on God.

It is vitally important that we know the difference between Spirit-led worship and the hypocrisy Jesus condemned in the Jews. Study the lists below, and meditate on the difference between these two:

Righteous Worship	Hypocritical Worship
From the heart	Feeds the flesh
Honors Christ	Magnifies man
Wins souls	Works to boast
Embraces humility	Produces pride
Reveals the love of God	Reveals the heart of man

Which of these characterize your worship? List them below.

_____

_____

_____

What does First John 4:10 teach about the Spirit?

_____

_____

_____

The gift of discerning of spirits is the ability to judge and separate a spirit of sincerity from a spirit of deception. This gift protects us from deception and false teachings. *Discerning the spirits* means being spiritually mature and prepared to know the difference between righteous worship and hypocritical worship. If what we experience in our worship is not found in the Word of God, then we should be careful not to fall prey to a potentially false doctrine. Many spirits are roaming about, lying to us, and trying to entice us to sin (fortune tellers, mediums, and so on).

Such spirits should be tried because God doesn't honor those things we use to uplift ourselves, control other's lives, or deceive others about God and His power.

To be a discerner of spirits we must divide, examine, investigate, and critique the words, actions, and characteristics of those who profess godliness.

According to this knowledge, are you a discerner of spirits?

⚓ Yes
⚓ No

What have you learned about your own worship from today's study?

_____

A New Desire

If you want to have a new desire to live for Jesus, study the Old Testament pattern for Spirit-led worship. Discuss what you learn on the lines below.

_____

_____

_____

_____

Daily Journal

Record what you have learned about God and about
yourself from today's lesson on the lines below.

_____

_____

_____

_____

_____

_____

Day 2: Worshiping in Truth

Jesus told the woman at the well that *all who worship Him must worship in spirit and in truth*. We cannot worship in spirit effectively unless we also worship in truth. Psalm 145:18 says, "The LORD is nigh unto all them that call upon him, to all that call upon him in truth." The word "truth" in this passage means, "trustworthiness, certainty, etc."[2]. Worship in truth requires us to place our trust in the Word of God only!

The word truth appears in the King James Version of the Bible 235 times. John 17:17 says, "Sanctify them through thy truth: thy word is truth." Jesus made this statement as He prayed to His Father for the disciples. Jesus knew the only way His people could worship Him effectively was for their lives to be set apart and made holy by the truth of God's Word.

Therefore, to worship in truth, we must totally stand on the Word of God.

We must believe it, live it, and let it be our guide for all of life's decisions.

Second Timothy 3:16 says, "All scripture is given by inspiration of God, and is profitable for doctrine, for reproof, for correction, for instruction in righteousness." Scripture is truth, and the truths it contains are illuminated to us through the anointing power of the Holy Spirit. Worship and truth are inseparable. The Holy Spirit teaches us truth; our responsibility is to apply that truth to our lives. Effective worship will then manifest itself in our lives.

The Holy Spirit is the third person of the Godhead. He lives inside the heart of each believer. He rightly divides the truth of God's Word to all who hunger and thirst for righteousness. God is known as our Father. Jesus is our Savior. The Holy Spirit is our Comforter.

---

2   Strong, James, LL.D, S.T.D., The New Strong's Exhaustive Concordance Of The Bible. (Nashville, TN: Thomas Nelson Publishers, 1990), P.1122, Heb. 571, p.11

These three are one in the Godhead. John 15:26 says, "But when the Comforter is come, whom I will send unto you from the Father, even the Spirit of truth, which proceedeth from the Father, he shall testify of me." John 16:13 also reveals the work of the truth and worship. It says, "Howbeit when he, the Spirit of truth, is come, he will guide you into all truth: for he shall not speak of himself; but whatsoever he shall hear, that shall he speak: and he will show you things to come."

The bottom line is this: we can only worship God in truth through the power of the Holy Spirit. Any worship that is not Spirit-led is not true worship, and God only honors true worship.

Only worship that is based on the Word of God is honorable in the eyes of God. God's Word teaches us that worship must be done from a sincere heart; worship does not come from a manmade ritual that produces a temporary, emotional experience. As we study God's Word more, we learn more of His truth that leads to sincere worship. Psalm 33:4 says, "For the word of the LORD is right; and all his works are done in truth."

If God's Word teaches obedience, then we also worship God through obedience. If God's Word teaches us to love, then we worship God through love. If God's Word teaches us to confess our sins, then confession is a form of worship. We know these things to be truth because God's Word commands us to do these things. Abiding in these things is abiding in truth, and abiding in truth manifests God's presence in our lives on a daily basis.

Jesus Christ gave His life so we could know the truth. Knowing the truth requires two things. First, we must be saved. Second, we must properly interpret the Word of God.

Jesus Christ is truth. If we know Him as our personal Savior, then His truth will release us from all deception, false doctrine, and unrighteous forms of worship if we'll only apply it to our lives. The work of the Holy Spirit is to teach us the difference between truth and deception. John 16:8–14 says:

> "And when he is come, he will reprove the world of sin,
> and of righteousness, and of judgment: Of sin, because
> they believe not on me; Of righteousness, because I go

to my Father, and ye see me no more; Of judgment, because the prince of this world is judged. I have yet many things to say unto you, but ye cannot bear them now. Howbeit when he, the Spirit of truth, is come, he will guide you into all truth: for he shall not speak of himself; but whatsoever he shall hear, that shall he speak: and he will show you things to come. He shall glorify me: for he shall receive of mine, and shall show it unto you.:"

If we want to know the difference between truth and deception, we must walk in the Spirit and not in the flesh. Study the list below to see if you are worshiping in truth.

Truth	Deception
Cleanses	Confuses
Prevails	Perverts
Honors	Hides
Heals	Harbors
Redeems	Rebels

According to John 16:8–11, what truths does the Holy Spirit reveal to us?

Where are we to go to find the truth?

What does Hebrews 4:12 says about the Word of God? Record the entire Scripture below.

A New Desire

Study Colossians 3:16. Record below what you learned about the Word of God and true worship from this Scripture.

_____

_____

_____

_____

_____

Daily Journal

Record below what you learned from today's
study about worshiping in truth.

_____

_____

_____

_____

_____

_____

_____

_____

Day 3: Getting in the Presence of God

Isaiah 57:15 says, "For thus saith the high and lofty One that inhabiteth eternity, whose name is Holy; I dwell in the high and holy place, with him also that is of a contrite and humble spirit, to revive the spirit of the humble, and to revive the heart of the contrite ones."

As God's children, we have His presence within us.

God is always faithful to make Himself known to us.

However, we must meet two conditions to recognize His presence. Those two conditions are found in the Scripture above. We must have a *humble and contrite spirit*. Brokenness (contrition) and lowliness (humility) usher in God's presence because they put us in a state of worship.

A contrite and humble spirit produces worship because it causes us to draw near to Him in sincerity, recognizing that He is our only hope. As we approach Him in this state, we have prepared our hearts for cleansing and purification. Hebrews 10:22 says, "Let us draw near with a true heart in full assurance of faith, having our hearts sprinkled from an evil conscience, and our bodies washed with pure water." This verse gives us several pointers to help prepare us for acceptable worship.

First it says, "Let us draw near with a sincere heart." We should come to God with a right heart of repentance and confession. We can't approach God while holding things back. God knows everything, and we should worship Him as an all-knowing God. We cannot enter the throne room of God with a heart of deception and hypocrisy.

Next we must draw near "with assurance of faith." The only acceptable worship to God is approaching Him in total faith. Faith in Jesus Christ is the only way to God.

Then we must have our hearts sprinkled from an evil conscience. Salvation by grace through faith gives us the confidence we need to approach God. However, sprinkling our hearts from an evil conscience means we also approach God with a sense of humility and unworthiness. It means we come to Him with the full awareness that we have no right to sit in His presence without the cleansing action of His blood in our hearts. The blood of Christ is the only absolute way to come into God's presence.

Salvation, sincerity, faith, and humility are the keys to entering God's presence. When we apply these four points to our lives, God honors our worship. We can enter His presence openly and honestly. We must enter His presence *holy* and *empty* by means of offering and sacrifice.

Jesus became the ultimate sacrificial offering to provide us with access to God. We too must approach Him with sacrifice in a total attitude of reverence and with a heart to worship. This is the only way we can sit in God's presence. Worship is a matter of the heart, not of the mind or emotions.

There are seven principles that define worship and bring us into the presence of God. As you apply each one of these principles, God will honor your sincerity. He draws to Himself those who come in true worship. He longs to revive the spirit of the humble and the heart of the contrite. John 4:23–24 says, "But the hour cometh, and now is, when the true worshippers shall worship the Father in spirit and in truth: for the Father seeketh such to worship him. God is a Spirit: and they that worship him must worship him in spirit and in truth."

Let's study these seven principles and allow God to revive us.

> **W**illingly come.
> **O**ffer yourself as an offering.
> **R**eadily repent.
> **S**ure of salvation.
> **H**onor Him.
> **I**nquire of Him.
> **P**ray powerfully.

1. Willingly Come

God wants us to approach Him willingly. He doesn't want to force us to worship Him. Whatever we do for God should be done for His glory, not for self-satisfaction. Psalm 95:6–7 says, "O come, let us worship and bow down: let us kneel before the LORD our maker. For he is our God; and we are the people of his pasture, and the sheep of his hand."

2. Offer an Offering

God wants us to approach Him with an offering. God requires the same offering from each of us as He did from Abraham—the giving of ourselves and everything about us (jobs, homes, children, spouses, wealth, poverty, sin, etc.) to Himself. First Chronicles 16:27–29 says, "Glory and honour are in his presence; strength and gladness are in his place. Give unto the LORD, ye kindreds of the people, give unto the LORD glory and strength. Give unto the LORD the glory due unto his name: bring an offering, and come before him: worship the LORD in the beauty of holiness." First Peter 2:4–5 says, "To whom coming, as unto a living stone, disallowed indeed of men, but chosen of God, and precious, Ye also, as lively stones, are built up a spiritual house, an holy priesthood, to offer up spiritual sacrifices, acceptable to God by Jesus Christ."

3. Readily Repent

God wants us to enter His presence with a spirit of repentance. This requires us to turn to God with a heart of confession and a willingness to change our attitude. True worship calls for self-examination, after which we turn to God for deliverance from the things that hinder our walk with Him.

A plea for help will draw God's attention
greater than anything else.

God stands ready to respond to all who call upon Him. Acts 3:19 says, "Repent ye therefore, and be converted, that your sins may be blotted out, when the times of refreshing shall come from the presence of the Lord."

4. Sure of Salvation

God does not hear the cries of a sinner. Therefore, you must cry out to Him first for the gift of salvation before you can experience the presence of God. If you know without a doubt that Jesus is your Savior, then you can sit in heavenly places with Him. The first thing the Father sees is the blood of Jesus applied to your life. If the blood has been applied, you cannot be denied, and God will surely manifest His presence to you. Ephesians 1:13–14 says, "In whom ye also trusted, after that ye heard the word of truth, the gospel of your salvation: in whom also after that ye believed, ye were sealed with that holy Spirit of promise, Which is the earnest of our inheritance until the redemption of the purchased possession, unto the praise of his glory."

5. Honor Him

God draws near to those who approach Him with reverence and adoration. He is worthy of all our attention. As we realize His authority and control of all things, we should submit to these with humility. Then God will make Himself known to us. To honor God is to fear Him. First Chronicles 16:25–30 says:

> "For great is the LORD, and greatly to be praised: he also is to be feared above all gods. For all the gods of the people are idols: but the LORD made the heavens. Glory and honour are in his presence; strength and gladness are in his place. Give unto the LORD, ye kindreds of the people, give unto the LORD glory and strength. Give unto the LORD the glory due unto his name: bring an offering, and come before him: worship the LORD in the beauty of holiness. Fear before him, all the earth: the world also shall be stable, that it be not moved."

6. Inquire of Him

God will enter the presence of all who seek Him.

Inquiring of God means to ask, seek, and knock. God knows the heart of each believer. He knows what you need, knows your faith to believe, and knows the sincerity of your inquiry. Isaiah 21:12 says, "The watchman said, The morning cometh, and also the night: if ye will inquire, inquire ye: return, come." First John 5:14–15 says, "And this is the confidence that we have in him, that, if we ask any thing according to his will, he heareth us: And if we know that he hear us, whatsoever we ask, we know that we have the petitions that we desired of him."

7. Pray Powerfully

As we approach God in prayer, He faithfully hears and opens His arms of love, mercy, and compassion. Prayer is the line of communication that keeps us connected with the will of God and places us in an attitude and spirit of worship. Prayer is not the way we tell God things He didn't know. Rather, it is an emptying of ourselves and a declaration before God of who we really are. Prayer is a releasing of the daily grind of life and a reconnection to the line of constant intimacy with Christ. Ephesians 6:18 says, "Praying always with all prayer and supplication in the Spirit, and watching thereunto with all perseverance and supplication for all saints." First Timothy 4:5 says, "For it is sanctified by the word of God and prayer." James 5:16 says, "Confess your faults one to another, and pray one for another, that ye may be healed. The effectual fervent prayer of a righteous man availeth much."

Would you say you are applying the majority of these seven principles most of the time?

❑ Yes
❑ No

Which of these seven principles do you need to apply more perfectly in your own life?

Based on the information you have just studied, how often would you say you experience the presence of the Lord?

A New Desire

If you want to have a new desire to live for Jesus, study the response of Moses as He stood in the presence of God in Exodus 3. Record below what you discover about entering into the presence of God.

_____

_____

_____

_____

_____

_____

Daily Journal

Record below what you have learned about God
and about yourself from today's lesson.

_____

_____

_____

_____

_____

_____

_____

_____

Day 4: How to Know You are in the Presence of God

In Genesis 28, Jacob had recently left Beersheba and gone toward Haran. After a long journey, he found a place to sleep for the night. In verse 12, Jacob dreamed of a ladder with angels of God ascending and descending on it. Verse 13 says, "And, behold, the LORD stood above it, and said, I am the LORD God of Abraham thy father, and the God of Isaac: the land whereon thou liest, to thee will I give it, and to thy seed." Then verse 15 says, "And, behold, I am with thee, and will keep thee in all places whither thou goest, and will bring thee again into this land; for I will not leave thee, until I have done that which I have spoken to thee of." Even in Jacob's dream, he was in the presence of God. Verse 16 says, "And Jacob awaked out of his sleep, and he said, Surely the LORD is in this place; and I knew it not."

There are other areas in Scripture where God's presence was among His people without their knowledge. For example, Mary Magdalene thought she was speaking to a gardener when she encountered the Lord at the empty tomb. John 20:14–15 says, "And when she had thus said, she turned herself back, and saw Jesus standing, and knew not that it was Jesus. Jesus saith unto her, Woman, why weepest thou? whom seekest thou? She, supposing him to be the gardener, saith unto him, Sir, if thou have borne him hence, tell me where thou hast laid him, and I will take him away."

The two disciples on the road to Emmaus failed to realize they were walking and talking with Jesus. Luke 24:15–16 says, "And it came to pass, that, while they communed together and reasoned, Jesus himself drew near, and went with them. But their eyes were holden that they should not know him."

My friends, we are so much like Jacob, Mary Magdalene, and the two disciples.

We often mistake the presence of God in our lives for something or someone else.

How many times have we mistaken Jesus for the gardener? Many times we mistakenly try to give God's glory to something or someone else, but God still gets all of the glory regardless of how hard we work in His service. Isaiah 48:11 says, "For mine own sake, even for mine own sake, will I do it: for how should my name be polluted? and I will not give my glory unto another."

Jesus approaches us in mysterious and unexpected ways. When we least expect Him to appear, He does. Just when life seems hopeless and we have convinced ourselves that God has abandoned us, He is nearer than ever before.

God is faithful to draw near to us, and He is faithful to allow us to recognize when we are sitting in His Presence. Before we can see Him, we must approach Him with an attitude of worship.

If we are approaching God with a sincere desire to worship Him in spirit and in truth, we will begin to recognize His presence throughout our daily walk. We will not give His glory to another. We will know Him immediately because the words we will hear, the things He will see us through, the joy we will experience, the persecutions we will overcome are only possible when God is present.

Knowing the difference between God's presence and Satan's deception is one of the greatest battles Christians face. First John 4:1 says, "Beloved, believe not every spirit, but try the spirits whether they are of God: because many false prophets are gone out into the world." Study the following list to determine if we have been entertaining the presence of God or the power of Satan.

God's Presence	Satan's Power
Produces righteousness	Presents religion
Confirms truth	Causes doubt
Manifests joy	Spreads sorrow
Convicts	Contradicts
Reveals love	Provokes hatred
Unites	Divides

Comforts	Confuses
Claims victory	Delivers defeat
Exercises praise	Produces depression
Edifies holiness	Demonstrates evil

Knowing when we are in the presence of God becomes very clear through the study of God's Word. John 15:3–5 says:

> "Now ye are clean through the word which I have spoken unto you. Abide in me, and I in you. As the branch cannot bear fruit of itself, except it abide in the vine; no more can ye, except ye abide in me. I am the vine, ye are the branches: He that abideth in me, and I in him, the same bringeth forth much fruit: for without me ye can do nothing."

We must abide in Christ if we are going to recognize His Presence in our lives.

Thus, we should strive to overcome the distractions of this life that cause us to miss or mistake God's presence among us.

The word abide in the previous Scripture means to remain in or *to stay attached to*. Before we can abide in the presence of the Lord, we must be born again. We are grafted into the family of God through the blood of Jesus Christ. We should strive to live as Jesus lived, in holiness and righteousness, which moves us into an attitude and life of worship.

There are seven principles for getting into God's presence. Once we've applied these seven principles, we can abide in the holy of holies with Christ, our King. We will recognize His will, and He will lovingly respond to our desire to draw near to Him. Remember, worship is the key to inviting God to manifest His holy presence. Worship should not be a way of life; it should *be* our life!

Search your heart to see if you're applying these seven principles for getting in the presence of God.

Walk uprightly
Openly confess

Restore the relationship
Spiritual stability
Hunger for holiness
Increase in intimacy
Persevere in persecution

1. Walk Uprightly

This means living a life that is pleasing to God. When we live a life that reflects godliness, we can say that God is ever near. He gives us the power to live as He lived. Colossians 1:10–13 says, "That ye might walk worthy of the Lord unto all pleasing, being fruitful in every good work, and increasing in the knowledge of God."

2. Openly Confess

Confession is admitting or agreeing with God that we are who we are and we do what we do. God's presence will always provoke self-examination. It exposes our sin, our hindrances, and our sincerity. First John 1:9 says, "If we confess our sins, he is faithful and just to forgive us our sins, and to cleanse us from all unrighteousness."

3. Restore the Relationship

Restoration means a renewing or revival of a broken or divided intimacy. When we have a desire to talk with God, serve Him, or feel His presence, we are experiencing His presence. Isaiah 51:10–12 says:

> "Art thou not it which hath dried the sea, the waters of the great deep; that hath made the depths of the sea a way for the ransomed to pass over? Therefore the redeemed of the LORD shall return, and come with singing unto Zion; and everlasting joy shall be upon their head: they shall obtain gladness and joy; and sorrow and mourning shall flee away. I, even I, am he that comforteth you: who art thou, that thou shouldest

be afraid of a man that shall die, and of the son of man which shall be made as grass."

4. Spiritual Stability

We must be rooted and unmovable in the truth of God's Word. Jesus is the Way, the Truth, and the Life. God's presence hovers around us when we stay true to Him in the midst of life's storms. First Corinthians 15:58 says, "Therefore, my beloved brethren, be ye steadfast, unmovable, always abounding in the work of the Lord, forasmuch as ye know that your labor is not in vain in the Lord."

5. Hunger for Holiness

This means we want to be like Jesus, walk like Jesus, and talk like Jesus. The more we hunger for His love, compassion, and forgiveness, the closer we draw to Him. As our hunger for Him grows, He draws closer and closer until He's feeding us from His own hand. First Peter 1:13–19 says:

> "Wherefore gird up the loins of your mind, be sober, and hope to the end for the grace that is to be brought unto you at the revelation of Jesus Christ; As obedient children, not fashioning yourselves according to the former lusts in your ignorance: But as he which hath called you is holy, so be ye holy in all manner of conversation; Because it is written, Be ye holy; for I am holy. And if ye call on the Father, who without respect of persons judgeth according to every man's work, pass the time of your sojourning here in fear: Forasmuch as ye know that ye were not redeemed with corruptible things, as silver and gold, from your vain conversation received by tradition from your fathers; But with the precious blood of Christ, as of a lamb without blemish and without spot."

6. Increase in Intimacy

We must know God more personally by spending private time with Him. Jesus got very personal with us when He took our place on Calvary. We will realize how closely He walks with us as we spend time with Him in prayer and in the Word. We will realize that He is ever-present in our lives. James 4:6–10 says:

> "But he giveth more grace. Wherefore he saith, God resisteth the proud, but giveth grace unto the humble. Submit yourselves therefore to God. Resist the devil, and he will flee from you. Draw nigh to God, and he will draw nigh to you. Cleanse your hands, ye sinners; and purify your hearts, ye double minded. Be afflicted, and mourn, and weep: let your laughter be turned to mourning, and your joy to heaviness. Humble yourselves in the sight of the Lord, and he shall lift you up."

7. Persevere in Persecution

We must stay with God and live a life of righteousness even through storms, trials, and tribulations. We should give God the glory when we find the strength to keep going even though we'd rather give up. He is our power to persevere! Ephesians 6:16-18 says:

> "Above all, taking the shield of faith, wherewith ye shall be able to quench all the fiery darts of the wicked. And take the helmet of salvation, and the sword of the Spirit, which is the word of God: Praying always with all prayer and supplication in the Spirit, and watching thereunto with all perseverance and supplication for all saints."

According to these principles, have you been guilty of mistaking God's presence for something or someone else? Are you giving God's glory to yourself or to someone or something else? The following things also signify God's Presence in our lives. Are you experiencing?

Peace	Brokenness	Contentment	Unworthiness
Conviction	Love	Joy	Forgiveness
Revival	Giving	Excitement	Desire

A New Desire

If you want to have a new desire to live for Jesus, study the dream of Jacob in Genesis 29 and record below what you learned about recognizing God's presence.

_____

_____

_____

_____

_____

Daily Journal

Record what you have learned about God and
about yourself from today's lesson.

_____

_____

_____

_____

_____

_____

_____

Day 5: What to Do in the Presence of God

If we study the Word of God from Genesis to Revelation, we will see the many people who experienced the presence of God. We will also see how they responded in His presence. All people respond differently to the presence of God according to their spiritual state and their understanding of who God is, His power, and His authority in their lives.

Those who have never been saved will respond to the presence of God with reservation and reluctance. As He convicts their hearts and woos them to the decision of salvation, they will experience fear, and they might run from God's convicting power.

Someone who is *born again* but living outside of God's will may respond to God's presence with limitations and excuses. They know what God wants them to do, but they are not ready to sacrifice or activate faith to live in the center of God's will. Therefore, when God passes by, they walk away from His presence instead of responding in obedience to His call.

Those who are in the center of God's will live and breathe just to feel His presence, to walk with Him, and to talk with Him each day. They recognize God's presence and are so in love with Him that their response is total surrender. These people do not live in sinless perfection; rather, they are people like Noah, Moses, Abraham, David, Ruth, Esther, Jeremiah, Paul, and John. They are *everyday* people with everyday problems. They've committed sin, experienced pain, and faced rejection. They often feel hopeless, abandoned, alone, unworthy, and useless (as did the Bible figures mentioned) at times. They can feel like they have no purpose or place in this life.

Yes, this group of people knows God's voice and can sense His presence. They live each day longing to feel His presence just one more time. Still, their faith is rooted in God's Word enough to know that if they never feel His Presence again, He has not left nor forsaken them.

We can learn what to do (or not do) in God's presence just by studying the lives of these biblical examples. Adam and Eve hid themselves from God's presence because of their sin. Moses removed his shoes in total reverence to the holiness of God. In fear, Jacob wrestled with the angel of the Lord all night. The children of Israel fell to their knees and bowed their faces to the ground. John *fell at His feet as dead* when he was given the revelation. David danced after spending time with God, and then he sang and praised God after witnessing God's presence and power. The woman at the well sat and listened to His words—and her life was changed forever. She confessed her sins right there in His presence and became a new creation in Christ. These are just a few who found themselves in the presence of God. The list could go on and on.

Psalm 95:2–3 says, "Let us come before his presence with thanksgiving, and make a joyful noise unto him with psalms. For the LORD is a great God, and a great King above all gods." We must come before the Lord with a thankful heart. We must give ourselves, our attitudes, and our possessions to Him.

God wants total surrender from us.
He wants our victories and our failures.

He is faithful to give us a new song as we come to Him in brokenness. Psalm 100:2–3 says, "Serve the LORD with gladness: come before his presence with singing. Know ye that the LORD he is God: it is he that hath made us, and not we ourselves; we are his people, and the sheep of his pasture."

We've learned how to get in the presence of God and how to recognize His presence. Now we must learn what to do in God's presence, and again we must go back to an attitude of worship. Psalm 46:10 explains in a simple way what to do in God's presence. It says, "Be still, and know that I am God: I will be exalted among the heathen, I will be exalted in the earth." We should simply be still and not do anything. We must be like the woman at the well and just listen and believe. Have faith in the things of God. This, my friend, is true worship.

The seven principles for what we should do in God's will are:

Worship Him
Obey Him
Rejoice in Him
Sing for Him
Humbly bow before Him
Idolize Him
Praise Him

1. Worship Him

This means giving God all you have. Pour yourself into Him by serving Him, loving Him, uplifting His Name, and depending upon Him. Psalm 29:2–4 says:

Give unto the LORD the glory due unto his name; worship the LORD in the beauty of holiness. The voice of the LORD is upon the waters: the God of glory thundereth: the LORD is upon many waters. The voice of the LORD is powerful; the voice of the LORD is full of majesty.

2. Obey Him

As you sit in God's presence, you will find yourself doing what He has called you to do. The quickest way to enter a spiritual desert is to disobey God. Acts 5:29 says, "Then Peter and the other apostles answered and said, We ought to obey God rather than men."

3. Rejoice in Him

The more you see God work in your life, the more you will rejoice in Him. You will realize that He is truly God almighty, the one who sees you through it all. Psalm 5:11–12 says, "But let all those that put their trust in thee rejoice: let them ever shout for joy, because thou defendest them: let them also that love thy name be joyful in thee. For thou,

LORD, wilt bless the righteous; with favour wilt thou compass him as with a shield."

4. Sing for Him

We have an opportunity to sing of His goodness for every move He makes in our lives. God expects us to sing songs of thanksgiving, making melody in our hearts to the Lord. Ephesians 5:19 says, "Speaking to yourselves in psalms and hymns and spiritual songs, singing and making melody in your heart to the Lord."

5. Humbly Bow before Him

We must come humbly before God, knowing we are unworthy to approach the throne of grace apart from His redeeming work at Calvary. We should praise Him for the blood of Jesus that makes us worthy to call upon our Savior. First Peter 5:5–9 says:

> "Likewise, ye younger, submit yourselves unto the elder. Yea, all of you be subject one to another, and be clothed with humility: for God resisteth the proud, and giveth grace to the humble. Humble yourselves therefore under the mighty hand of God, that he may exalt you in due time: Casting all your care upon him; for he careth for you. Be sober, be vigilant; because your adversary the devil, as a roaring lion, walketh about, seeking whom he may devour: Whom resist stedfast in the faith, knowing that the same afflictions are accomplished in your brethren that are in the world."

6. Idolize Him

God should be our idol. We should put nothing before Him. He deserves our all. Put Him first in all of your life. Let nothing stand between you and God. Matthew 10:37–38 says, "He that loveth father or mother more than me is not worthy of me: and he that loveth son or daughter more than me is not worthy of me. And he that taketh not his cross, and followeth after me, is not worthy of me." Matthew 6:33 says, "But seek ye first the kingdom of God, and his righteousness; and all these things shall be added unto you."

7. Praise Him

As we bask in God's presence, we should lift up holy hands with praise and adoration. Praising Him requires a life unashamed of the gospel and a willingness to testify of His glorious works in our lives. Psalm 117:1–2 says, "O praise the LORD, all ye nations: praise him, all ye people. For his merciful kindness is great toward us: and the truth of the LORD endureth for ever. Praise ye the LORD."

What are you doing as you sit in the presence of God? Are you running, hiding, obeying, or rebelling?

_____

_____

_____

_____

_____

_____

_____

_____

_____

_____

_____

_____

A New Desire

If you want to have a new desire to live for Jesus, study the Old Testament preparations for worship and record below the difference in what they had to do back then and what we must do today to enter into God's presence.

_____

_____

_____

_____

_____

Daily Journal

Record what you've learned about God and
about yourself from today's lesson.

_____

_____

_____

_____

_____

_____

_____

_____

Endorsements

I thank God every day for inspiring Dr. Brenda Robinson to write *A New Desire*. I accepted Jesus Christ as my personal Savior after sitting under the teachings of this study. Shortly thereafter, my family and I left our home in Kansas and moved to Georgia to volunteer in New Desire Christian Ministries and serve God on a daily basis. I would recommend this study to anyone who would like to further his or her walk with the Lord and obtain a deeper relationship with Jesus Christ.

—Julie McNeil, Dental Hygienist

Upon the realization that I needed to grow closer in my daily walk with Christ, I began to want a Bible study book. I did not want just another ordinary study book; I wanted one that taught and corresponded with the Bible, provided study helps to apply in my daily life, would increase my effectiveness for Him, and would not be over my head while making me dig deeper in the Bible. God knew exactly what I needed, and He placed *A New Desire* by Dr. Brenda J. Robinson in my hands. Words cannot begin to describe how amazing this study was for my life. This workbook transformed how I study, pray, deal with issues of doubt, and view the power of God's love and the need to be living in God's will. I would recommend *A New Desire* to any brother or sister in Christ who wants a closer, more intimate relationship with Him.

—Kristi Turley, Educator

I have been privileged to witness the effectiveness of this work, *A New Desire*, since it was nothing more than a typed document in three-ring binders. I traveled across the Southeast with Dr. Robinson as she taught this work to Bible study groups, and I watched as people's lives were transformed by the biblical truth contained therein.

I have also had the awesome privilege of teaching these lessons to my personal Bible study groups and Sunday school classes. Each time I've heard it, read it, or taught it, I have been reminded of my own need to set sail daily on my own journey with Christ as I watched others grow and learn in the Word with me.

This is an outstanding Bible study that I would recommend to anyone who wants to take his or her walk with Christ to the next level!

—*Karen Tinsley Nelson*
Former Personal Assistant
To Brenda J. Robinson

Bibliography

Barnhart, Clarence L., Barnhart, Robert, eds. The World Book Dictionary. (Chicago, London, Sydney, Toronto: World Book, Inc., 1988)

Holy Bible: King James Version. (Nashville, TN: Thomas Nelson Publishers, 1990), The New Open Bible

New American Standard Bible. (La Habra, CA: The , 1960, 1962, 1963, 1968, 1971, 1972, 1973, 1975, 1995 by The Lockman Foundation)

Strong, James, LL.D, S.T.D., The New Strong's Exhaustive Concordance Of The Bible. (Nashville, TN: Thomas

Tenney, Merrill C., Steven Barabas, Th.D., Peter DeVisser., eds. The Zondervan Pictorial Bible Dictionary. (Grand Rapids, Michigan: Regency Reference Library of Zondervan Publishing House, 1963, 1964, 1967)

Webster's Pocket Dictionary And Thesaurus Of The English Language, New Revised Edition. (Allied Publishing Group, Inc., of Nichols Publishing Group 1999)

CPSIA information can be obtained at www.ICGtesting.com
Printed in the USA
LVOW042305120412

277398LV00002B/4/P